FOR THE GOOD OF MANKIND?

THE SHAMEFUL HISTORY OF HUMAN MEDICAL EXPERIMENTATION

VICKI ORANSKY WITTENSTEIN

TWENTY-FIRST CENTURY BOOKS / MINNEAPOLIS

For Andy, whose love and support inspire me — V.O.W.

I gratefully acknowledge the medical bioethicists who provided invaluable time and assistance in researching this book:

Arthur Caplan, Ph.D., Director of the Division of Medical Ethics, Department of Population Health at NYU Langone Medical Center; Karen J. Maschke, Ph.D., Research Scholar at the Hastings Center and editor of *IRB: Ethics & Human Research;* and Jerry Menikoff, M.D., J.D., Director, Office for Human Research Protections (OHRP).

Eva Mozes Kor very generously helped with details of her experience as a twin subjected to experiments at Auschwitz. May the story of this extraordinary woman continue to remind us that science should never cast away its ethical principles.

I especially want to thank my editor Domenica Di Piazza, whose keen intelligence and interest in the topic sparked my enthusiasm and guided me through the project. Thanks, too, to my agent, Brianne Johnson, for all her support.

I greatly appreciate my family of cheerleaders: my husband, Andy; and Ted, Alyssa, and Lily Wittenstein; Amanda and Jeff Shackelton; and Millicent Nathan. A special shout-out goes to my friend and colleague, Diana Childress.

Twenty-First Century Books
A division of Lerner Publishing Group, Inc.
241 First Avenue North
Minneapolis, MN 55401 U.S.A.

Website address: www.lernerbooks.com

Library of Congress Cataloging-in-Publication Data

Wittenstein, Vicki O., 1954–
        For the Good of Mankind? : the shameful history of human medical
    experimentation / by Vicki Oransky Wittenstein.
            page   cm.
        Includes bibliographical references and index.
        ISBN 978-1-4677-0659-9 (lib. bdg. : alk. paper)
        ISBN 978-1-4677-1661-1 (eBook)
        1. Human experimentation in medicine–History. 2. Medical sciences—
    Research—Methodology—History. I. Title.
    R853.H8W58 2014
    174.2'8—dc23   2012043413

Manufactured in the United States of America
1 – CG – 7/15/13

TABLE OF CONTENTS

Simeon Shaw on his mother's lap in 1946. The Shaws came to the United States from Australia seeking cancer treatment for Simeon, who was instead injected with radioactive plutonium. His doctors did not seek informed consent from the family. Secret experiments such as this continued for decades in the United States.

INTRODUCTION

One day in January 1946, Simeon Shaw, a four-year-old boy known as Simmy, fell out of a hammock on the porch of his home in Dubbo, Australia, and broke his leg. X-rays revealed that Simmy also had a serious form of bone cancer. According to the doctor, Simmy had less than a year to live.

His parents were devastated. They frantically sought other medical opinions and contacted the American Red Cross for help. Doctors at the University of California Hospital in San Francisco (UCSF) heard about Simmy's plight and agreed to treat him. The U.S. Army stepped in to help as well. Soldiers in the Pacific region, flying home from recently ended World War II (1939–1945), gladly gave up their seats for Simmy and his mother, Freda Shaw. Mother and son flew more than 10,000 miles (16,000 kilometers) to San Francisco in an army transport plane.

The media loved the story. Newspaper headlines proclaimed, "Mercy Flight Brings Aussie Boy Here" and "Specialists Hope to Cure Boy, 4." "I just can't express how kind the Red Cross and the Air Forces have been," Freda Shaw said to the reporters and photographers at the San Francisco airstrip.

Unknown to the Shaws, the doctors at UCSF were part of a secret military experiment to test the effects of radiation on the human body. Curing Simmy was not what the doctors had in mind. They instead injected Simmy with toxic radioactive substances, including plutonium. His mother was not told about the injections and never gave consent. The doctors then performed a bone biopsy on Simmy's leg. Bone, muscle, and tissue specimens were analyzed to track the absorption of radiation from the injections.

"I JUST CAN'T EXPRESS HOW KIND THE RED CROSS AND THE AIR FORCES HAVE BEEN."—FREDA SHAW, MOTHER OF SIMMY SHAW, 1946

Simmy returned to Australia after several months, but by that time, his cancer had spread, and he was weaker. He died about nine months after the injections.

Almost seventy years have elapsed since the military conducted its secret radiation experiments on Simmy and hundreds of others. But these serious breaches of medical ethics still cast a shadow over the history of human experimentation. In most cases, people didn't understand the risks involved. Often no one bothered to explain. Tragically, many people died.

Over the past 150 years, doctors and scientists have achieved huge medical advances. Cures and treatments abound due to the availability of antibiotics and other medicines, screening tests, and surgeries. But these discoveries have come at a price—frequent violations of the rights of human participants.

In the twenty-first century, laws in the United States protect people who are subjects in experiments, but problems remain. Thousands of volunteers fill the ever-growing number of legally required research studies, called clinical trials. In the rush to get new products to the market for financial gain and to develop new treatments, vaccinations, and techniques, abuses and ethical lapses still occur.

Government agencies find it difficult to oversee the vast number of clinical trials in the United States, as well as in poor countries around the world. Laws don't always protect participants in newer areas of research, such as genetic therapies. Clearly, though, human experimentation is critical. Someone has to be tested first. Who should it be? Is it fair to give the treatment to prison inmates, the mentally ill, or children? What about people for whom there is no cure or healthy people who are willing to participate for money? How can we best protect the rights of individuals while encouraging important medical discoveries?

Scientific and medical discoveries of the twenty-first century offer the promise of a future without serious medical conditions. Society must continue to experiment on humans to find new treatments and cures. In balancing the rights of the individual versus the advancement of science and medicine, how will you decide between what is right and wrong?

CHAPTER ONE

CREATING HUMAN GUINEA PIGS

The little children would lie in their beds moaning all night from
the pain in their eyes. They kept their little hands pressed over
their eyes, unable to sleep from the sensations they had to
undergo. Water would stream from their eyes so continually that
deep grooves formed on the sides of their faces.

—Diana Belais, supporter of abolishing human experimentation, reporting on experiments with
orphans, 1910

In the above account, a nurse at St. Vincent's Home for Orphans in
Philadelphia, Pennsylvania, described the pain children endured from
experimental eye injections in 1908. In those days, tuberculosis ran
rampant in cities. The injections were part of an experiment to find a way
to diagnose the disease, which usually affects the lungs. Three doctors
introduced tuberculosis toxin (called tuberculin) into the eyes of about
160 healthy children under the age of eight, including 17 infants.

The doctors saw nothing wrong with the experiments. In published
journals, they openly discussed the children's discomfort. In describing the
case of an orphan called Little Catharine, the Philadelphia doctors wrote:
"After the tuberculin was placed in her eye, the lid became swollen to large
proportions and fell half way down her cheek. This enormous lid, covering
the entire eye, under which pus continued to gather, taxed to the utmost
the skill of the physicians....It seemed impossible to relieve the little one."

According to the doctors, a number of the children would most likely
suffer permanent eye injury. In their report, the doctors acknowledged
other experiments where children had similar reactions to the eye solution.
And a year later, a New York City doctor wrote about conducting a similar
experiment with one thousand children at Babies' Hospital. Eventually,

doctors decided against using the tuberculin test. But this did not stop the practice of dangerous and cruel experimentation.

From the late 1700s to the 1940s, U.S. doctors experimented not only on orphans but also on other powerless people, such as African American slaves, the poor, and the mentally ill. People confined in hospitals, prisons, and other institutions were also targets. How and why did human beings become guinea pigs?

The Hippocratic Oath

Throughout history, people have tried to understand how the human body works and to diagnose and cure disease. In ancient times, the Hippocratic Oath governed a doctor's responsibilities. Hippocrates was a doctor who lived in Greece during the fifth century B.C.E. The oath, which was written about 470 to 360 B.C.E., listed the ethical principles to be followed by doctors. The fundamental principle is "*Primum non nocere,*" which is Latin for "First of all, to do no harm."

For most of early history, practicing sound medicine was not distinguishable from experimenting. Although some doctors stepped over the line and experimented on people for the sake of science, doctors mostly followed the teachings of Hippocrates. They observed the course of a disease, consulted with other doctors, and attempted various cures. New treatments were offered when others failed. In other words, experiments were mostly conducted for *therapeutic* purposes, where doctors intended a direct benefit for the patient.

But in an effort to find cures for diseases such as smallpox that killed and scarred vast numbers of people, doctors began engaging in riskier experiments on healthy people in the 1700s. They often used children, who hadn't yet been exposed to the diseases.

Smallpox

More than one hundred years before poor Little Catharine was injected with tuberculin, Edward Jenner, an English doctor, experimented with smallpox. His subject was an eight-year-old boy, James Phipps, who was the son of Jenner's gardener.

After scratching James's arm, Jenner rubbed in material from a cowpox sore on a dairymaid's hand. (Cowpox is a mild infection caused by a virus similar to smallpox.) James got mildly sick with cowpox. A month later, Jenner scratched the boy's arm again, but this time, he rubbed in material from a deadly smallpox scab. He later repeated the smallpox experiment on James, but the boy never got sick. Jenner had shown that cowpox could

Edward Jenner vaccinated several children (including his infant son, as shown in this illustration from 1815) in his experiments with smallpox. In 1798 he published the results of his successful work but met with much ridicule. Many people, especially in the church, felt it was wrong to vaccinate humans with matter derived from diseased animals. However, because of the protection they provided, smallpox vaccinations were soon widely accepted.

immunize (protect) people against smallpox.

It's not clear whether James Phipps consented to Jenner's experiment. James was young. And since James's father worked for Jenner, his parents would likely have felt obligated to participate. But in the 1800s and the 1900s, consent for a medical treatment given to children or adults was not judged in the same way as it is today. Modern laws require that doctors giving medical treatment first obtain consent from their subjects.

Back then, though, there were no laws about experimentation. Although many of the experiments bordered on nontherapeutic, doctors were allowed much greater leeway in trying new treatments for so-called therapeutic or preventive reasons. In 1865 a French physiologist, Claude Bernard, wrote that doctors had a moral obligation to experiment on humans before they adopted new treatments. He also affirmed the Hippocratic mandate to "do no harm," even if an experiment might advance scientific knowledge.

Yet, Bernard did not think it was wrong to experiment on a woman who was to be put to death. He considered the dying person, whether from an illness or from punishment, in a different category. In the case discussed by Bernard, the condemned woman was forced to swallow worm larvae. After her death, her intestines were checked to see if the worms had grown. Bernard reasoned that the woman was not a patient. She was the subject of an experiment.

Obtaining Consent

How did doctors recruit volunteers and obtain consent for an experiment? And did the ethics of the time demand that physicians always tell patients the truth? In 1803 an English physician named Thomas Percival wrote in his well-known book, *Medical Ethics,* that honesty was second to therapeutic care.

Percival wrote that the patient's right to know the truth "is suspended, and even annihilated" if it negatively affects the patient, his family, or even the community. Percival's view was endorsed by the American Medical Association (AMA) in its first code of ethics in 1847. The idea that a doctor need not tell a patient the truth carried throughout the 1800s.

Doctors frequently offered payment of some sort when the experiments were particularly risky. For example, Alexis St.

Martin, a French Canadian trapper, was accidentally shot in the stomach in 1822. William Beaumont, a surgeon in the U.S. Army, stitched up St. Martin's wound. But he was unable to close it entirely. Food and stomach liquids dripped out of the hole.

Beaumont decided to take advantage of the situation to learn about how humans digest food. St. Martin was paid a yearly salary of $150 to take part in Beaumont's experiments. He also received food, clothing, and a place to live. For the study, Beaumont added foods into the hole in St. Martin's stomach and then removed them. He subjected St. Martin to different diets and fasting.

But St. Martin was clearly miserable. People poked fun of "the man without a stomach." Years later, St. Martin suffered further humiliation at the hands of a medical practitioner named T. G. Bunting. For several years, Bunting displayed St. Martin and his stomach to curiosity seekers in the eastern United States and Canada.

African American Medical Wonders

From the late eighteenth century to the early twentieth century, exhibiting the subjects of human experiments in the United States and Europe was not uncommon. This was particularly true of African American slaves. Pygmies from Africa, a "giant" African woman, and a black man whose skin was turning white are just a few of the examples. The medical community and the general public flocked to these exhibits. Scientists and doctors interested in theories about race and evolution came to observe how the black body differed from the white. The demeaning exhibits confirmed unjust beliefs about the alleged inferiority of black people.

These displays had the appeal of a circus, particularly when the famous U.S. circus man P. T. Barnum got in on the act. One of Barnum's most famous displays was Joice Heth, a black slave whom he purchased in 1835. Heth had very black, wrinkled skin, no teeth or eyes, and was paralyzed in her legs and one arm. After Heth died, Barnum paid a New York surgeon to dissect Heth's body in public. Fifteen hundred people paid fifty cents a ticket to see the sight.

If you were a black slave at this time, though, you weren't paid to be part of a medical experiment, and no one asked you for consent. Instead, doctors paid the slave owners to experiment on you. Some doctors even bought slaves with particular medical conditions just so they could test new treatments.

One U.S. doctor, who conducted particularly gruesome experiments on slaves in Alabama, was the well-known surgeon

This handbill from 1835 advertises an exhibition of Joice Heth in P. T. Barnum's winter circus in his hometown of Bridgeport, Connecticut. With her physical disabilities, Heth was considered an object of curiosity, which people were willing to pay to see.

James Marion Sims. He cut open the skulls of black infants, for example, to find a treatment for tetany, a condition that caused severe muscle spasms in plantation children. With a cobbler's tools, he forced apart skull bones, mistakenly believing that the shifting of the bones during childbirth caused tetany.

Sims performed even more horrifying surgeries on slave women. Many slaves who had problems during childbirth were left unable to control their urine and feces. Hoping to find

WITH A COBBLER'S TOOLS, SIMS FORCED APART SKULL BONES.

a cure for this condition, known as vesicovaginal fistula, Sims operated experimentally on several slave women in the 1840s. He even operated thirty times on one slave named Anarcha. Although he knew about the discovery of ether as an anesthesia to dull pain, Sims refused to use it. Sims did find a cure and eventually perfected the surgical technique. He was heralded as the father of American gynecology. Sims received many honors, and statues around the world were erected in his name.

Most physicians did not object to experiments performed for the "treatment" of slaves. Yet, they did debate about what was right and wrong when it came to other kinds of people and experiments. In 1874 an experiment on a feebleminded thirty-year-old named Mary Rafferty was highly criticized. Doctors in Ohio had unsuccessfully treated cancer on her scalp with surgery. When Dr. Roberts Bartholow realized that Rafferty was going to die, he seized the opportunity to conduct a series of painful electrode experiments in her brain. As the electric current ran through her exposed brain, Rafferty writhed in pain and cried out. An autopsy after Rafferty's death revealed brain damage.

Bartholow was severely reprimanded by the AMA for violating a physician's ethical duty not to harm his patient. Scientific experimentation was not a justification for injury. Bartholow claimed that Rafferty had consented. But many critics questioned the meaning of consent from a mentally challenged person.

Doctors Become Scientists

The confusion over consent and the boundaries between experiments and treatment continued to plague doctors throughout the nineteenth century. By the 1870s, new scientific knowledge of bacteria, drugs, and vaccines spurred demands for human experimentation. Doctors were excited about innovative technologies, such as X-rays and stomach tubes. Suddenly, there were promising new treatments and cures. And humans were needed to test them.

The doctor's role became forever transformed. No longer was a physician simply a practitioner who observed and attempted various cures. Now the ideal doctor was a scientist. His authority and knowledge came from experimentation.

In addition, doctors could take advantage of a new institution—medical hospitals—for experiments. Before the Civil War (1861–1865), hospitals were places only for sick and helpless poor people. After the war, they became institutions of medical science.

Middle- and upper-class people, who had preferred the privacy of their own bedroom or a doctor's office, began to go to hospitals. Between 1873 and 1909, the number of hospitals in the United States grew from 178 to 4,359. And as hospitals grew, so did horror stories about them. For example, African Americans told of "night doctors" who swooped up black people from the street and brought them to hospitals for experimentation.

The Antivivisection Movement

In the late 1800s, antivivisectionists took up the cause against human experimentation. Antivivisectionists were against performing experimental surgery on living creatures. They were already against the use of animals in laboratory experiments. They feared that the rapid growth of science would push doctors to experiment on humans in order to gain scientific knowledge rather than to find cures.

Antivivisectionist societies sprang up in cities across the United States. Antivivisectionists, such as Dr. Albert T. Leffingwell, a well-known advocate for humane experimentation, were particularly incensed by the yellow fever experiments conducted by Italian bacteriologist Giuseppe Sanarelli in 1897. Yellow fever is a tropical disease that killed many American soldiers during the Spanish-American War of 1898. The disease was also prevalent in the southern United States. After the Philippines and Cuba—which both have tropical climates—became U.S. territories, scientists vigorously searched for a cure.

Sanarelli mistakenly thought he had found the germ that caused the disease. He injected five hospital patients with a solution containing the inactivated (not alive) germ—without their consent. Although none of the five died, they all became violently ill with high fevers, dizziness, and vomiting. The experiments brought cries for laws prohibiting human experimentation for scientific purposes. Critics denounced the idea that science be placed above the needs of the patient.

Yellow Fever and Informed Consent

By the early 1900s, researchers had started to find methods to avoid using people as uninformed guinea pigs. Researchers faced less criticism by experimenting on themselves, obtaining written consent from volunteers, or paying experimental subjects. The yellow fever experiments led by U.S. Army physician Walter Reed in 1900 were a famous example that used all three strategies.

Enlisted medical personnel from the Hospital Corps at Camp Columbia in Havanna, Cuba, volunteered to participate in Walter Reed's yellow fever experiments in 1900. They were among the first subjects in the history of medical experimentation to provide written consent.

Major Reed sailed to Cuba to test whether a mosquito was the carrier of yellow fever. Before experimenting on others, Reed's team of doctors decided to be the first subjects of their own experiment. After being bitten by the mosquitoes, two of the doctors, James Carroll and Jesse Lazear, became desperately ill. Lazear died. (Reed, who was back in Washington, D.C., at this time, did not experiment on himself.)

Despite Lazear's death, U.S. servicemen and Spanish immigrants volunteered. Because of the dangers, Reed required the volunteers to sign a written consent form before he would allow them to participate. He also paid them each $100 in gold, plus an additional $100 if the subject got sick. Free medical care was also provided in the event a subject became ill. A few men, though, refused payment and volunteered in the hope of finding a cure.

The experiments proved that mosquitoes carry the deadly yellow fever virus. Reed was hailed for the discovery, and his name was forever linked to the courage of the doctors who risked their lives for medicine. His experiment also marked an important step in protecting human subjects— voluntary written consent. Also significant was the idea that healthy people could be subjected to experiments, as long as they understood the dangers.

Experimenting on Children, Prisoners, and Soldiers

Many medical experiments of the early 1900s took advantage of children. For example, in 1911 Hideyo Noguchi, a microbiologist at Rockefeller Institute in New York City, disclosed his attempts to develop a test for syphilis, a sexually transmitted disease. After first experimenting on animals and then on himself and other physicians, Noguchi enlisted the support of fifteen doctors to obtain a group of four hundred people. Forty-six of the healthy volunteers were orphans, some as young as two years old. One hundred other children and adults were patients hospitalized for other illnesses. None of these volunteers gave their consent to the testing, which involved injections of luetin, a solution containing an inactive form of the spirochete (bacterium) that causes syphilis.

Although none of the volunteers became ill from the luetin, antivivisectionists were outraged, particularly with respect to the use of orphans who had no parent or legal guardian to protect them. The Vivisection Investigation League circulated a pamphlet stating, "Are the helpless people in our hospitals, and asylums to be treated as so much material for scientific experimentation, irrespective of age or consent?" The New York Society for the Prevention of Cruelty to Children pressed

THE HUMAN GUINEA PIG

Vivisection literally means "cutting into a live organism." But in the 1800s, the term was used for all kinds of experimentation involving both animals and humans. In 1913 a noted antivivisectionist was the famous Irish playwright George Bernard Shaw. Shaw first coined the expression "human guinea pig." He wrote about the "folly which sees in the child nothing more than the vivisector sees in a guinea pig: something to experiment on with a view to rearranging the world."

assault charges against Noguchi, but the Manhattan District Attorney's Office refused to prosecute the case.

Infants at a New York City orphanage were the uninformed subjects of another later experiment. To learn more about scurvy, a disease caused by lack of vitamin C, researchers withheld orange juice from babies until they developed symptoms of the disease. After the infants were cured, researchers withheld the juice a second time to see if the orphans would contract the disease again.

Editors of a professional medical journal, *American Medicine,* responded to the public outrage. They wrote that the scurvy tests did not exploit the children but instead gave the orphans the opportunity to contribute "a large return to the community for the

care devoted to them." Although apparently some of the infants did not completely recover, the harm to the children was viewed as minimal, and the trade-off was thought to be acceptable.

Concerns also surfaced about experimenting on prisoners and people serving in the military. In 1915 researchers put twelve inmates at a Mississippi prison on a six-month diet of corn syrup, biscuits, pork, and corn bread. They wanted to see if the poor diet would bring on pellagra, a deadly disease caused by a deficiency of vitamin B_3. The governor of Mississippi had guaranteed that he would set the prisoners free if they volunteered for the experiment. He also offered them free medical care upon release.

Antivivisectionists viewed the governor's payment as nothing less than coercion. Diana Belais, the well-known antivivisectionist, wrote that prisoners could not "self-sacrifice for the good of medical science" in the same way that a free man could.

Medical experimentation on soldiers usually required voluntary consent. Yet, during World War I (1914–1918), U.S. military surgeons removed the gallbladders of servicemen who were carriers of typhoid. Doctors thought the operations would stop the dreaded disease. The men were forced to comply or face punishment for military crimes.

In the years before the outbreak of World War II, researchers were frantic to find cures for childhood diseases such as polio and measles. The vaccinations were tested, again on orphans. For some experiments, however, parents were asked to give consent for their children. This practice raised new questions: Was it okay for parents to volunteer their children? What about an infant? What were the acceptable age limits for testing on children?

In the 1930s, pathologist John A. Kolmer tested the live polio virus on animals, then on himself and his two children. Twenty-three other children also received the virus, with the consent of their parents.

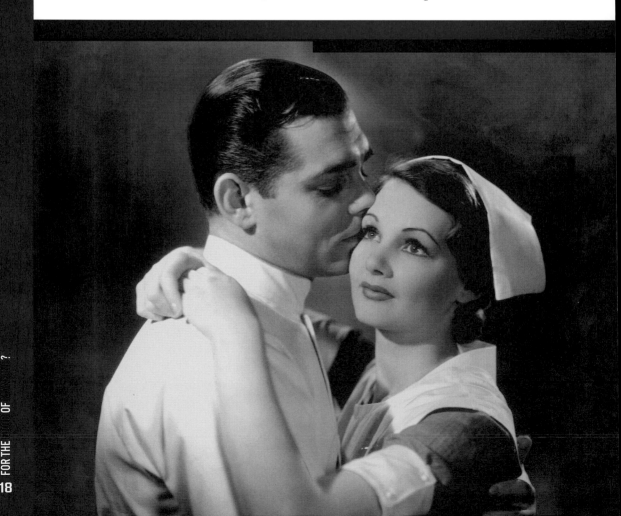

Eventually, three hundred more children were vaccinated. Nine of the children died. Americans panicked, and because of the horror of the deaths of the children, live polio vaccines wouldn't be tested again until 1956.

Abusers or Heroes?

Most Americans were genuinely outraged when doctors overstepped the boundaries of human experimentation. Without a doubt, serious abuses had occurred. But generally, the many new treatments and cures sparked confidence in doctors, medicine, and science. The medical profession was held in high esteem, and experimenting doctors were seen as heroes.

Throughout the years, doctors had resisted attempts to enact laws restricting experimentation. They feared formal laws would stop the advancement of medical science and treatments. The doctors also worried that restrictions might expose them to legal action. In general, doctors thought they could regulate the ethics of experimentation themselves.

Then came World War II. The atrocities committed in the name of science during this conflict would change forever the way medical science approached experimentation on human subjects.

DOCTORS, HEROES OF MEDICAL SCIENCE

In the 1930s, popular movies such as *Men in White*, starring Clark Gable, and *Yellow Jack*, starring Robert Montgomery, praised physicians and researchers. *Yellow Jack*, which featured the heroes of the yellow fever experiments, including those who had volunteered, also became a Broadway play starring Jimmy Stewart. The Metro-Goldwyn-Mayer movie-making company produced short movies highlighting the discoveries of real-life doctors such as Louis Pasteur, Frederick Banting, and Charles Best. Medical journalist Paul de Kruif wrote about the scientists, doctors, and technicians who pioneered discoveries in the study of bacteria and other microbes in his 1926 book *Microbe Hunters*. Sinclair Lewis's 1925 novel *Arrowsmith* also celebrated medical scientists and was made into a movie.

Clark Gable *(far left)* and Elizabeth Allan *(left)* starred in *Men in White*, a 1934 film about an affair between Dr. George Ferguson, a committed young doctor, and Barbara Dennin, the nurse who shares his unfailing dedication to patients.

Eva Mozes *(far left)* and her twin sister Miriam *(in back, next to Eva)* were among the many Jewish victims of Josef Mengele, a Nazi doctor at Auschwitz, where they were interned during World War II. This photo was taken in 1945 when the camp was liberated.

CHAPTER TWO

NAZI CRIMES AGAINST HUMANITY

I hope that what was done to me will never again happen to another human being. . . .Scientists should continue to do research. But if a human being is ever used in the experiments, the scientists must make a moral commitment never to violate a person's human rights and human dignity.

—Eva Mozes Kor, Nazi concentration camp survivor, 1992

In the spring of 1944, German Nazi soldiers rounded up ten-year-old Eva Mozes and her family from their home in Transylvania, Romania, and forced them to board a cattle car train. They were transported from their rural village to Birkenau (sometimes referred to as Auschwitz II), a Nazi concentration camp in Poland. Eva could "smell the stench of the cramped bodies." The family's only crime was that they were Jewish.

When Eva arrived at the camp, the doors of the cattle car flung open. Soldiers shoved families apart, separating the men from the women. Those who didn't cooperate were shot dead. Eva's father and two older sisters were swept up in the crowd. A soldier pulled Eva and her identical twin sister, Miriam, to one side of the railroad platform. A second soldier dragged their mother in a different direction. Eva never saw her mother, father, or two older sisters again.

Jews who were strong enough to work in the concentration camps survived—at least until they fell ill or became too frail to work. Those who were weak or old and children were immediately killed. Many were murdered in gas chambers. Others were burned to death in ovens called crematoriums. But because they were twins, Eva and Miriam were not put to death at Birkenau. Their lives were spared for one purpose: human medical experimentation. No one ever explained to Eva and Miriam what would be done to them. No one ever considered ways to minimize their pain. Because the children were Jews, the doctors did what they pleased. In fact, many of the experiments were performed to prove that Jews were inferior.

Dr. Josef Mengele

Dr. Josef Mengele was the most notorious of about thirty doctors who conducted research at Auschwitz. Mengele studied twins like Eva and Miriam as well as people with disabilities. Anyone who was a dwarf, had a hunchback, or was otherwise deformed was fair game. Mengele also was interested in hair color and people who had eyes of different colors. He collected eyeballs from those on whom he experimented and tried to figure out if it was possible to change a person's eye color. When the war was over, Eva wrote a personal account of the horror she endured as part of Mengele's experiments. She said:

> To look back at my childhood is to remember my experiences as a human guinea pig in the Birkenau laboratory of Dr. Josef Mengele. To recount such painful memories is to relive the horrors of human experimentation, where people were used as merely objects or means to a scientific end. I envision the chimneys, the smell of burning flesh, the medical injections, the endless blood taking, the tests, the dead bodies all around us, the hunger, and the rats. Nothing that is close to human existence existed in that place.

Mengele conducted two types of experiments on twins. One type traced the genetic origins of certain diseases. The second was related to how germs would spread if used for warfare. Identical twins, who carry the same genetic makeup, were ideal subjects for understanding the relationship between heredity and the environment.

A few months after the girls arrived at Birkenau, doctors under Mengele's supervision injected Eva with a germ that made her desperately ill. She tried to hide her high temperature from them. She knew they would separate her from Miriam if she got sick. Instead, the doctors sent her to the camp hospital. "I was placed in a barrack filled with moving and screaming skeletons," Eva wrote later. "Twice a week a

"TWICE A WEEK A TRUCK WOULD COME TO PICK UP THE LIVING DEAD."
—EVA MOZES KOR, 1992

Dr. Josef Mengele *(second from left, with arms crossed)* at Auschwitz with other members of a branch of the Nazi Schutzstaffel, or SS, who served in the concentration camps during World War II. Some of Mengele's horrific experiments focused on twins such as Eva and her sister.

truck would come to pick up the living dead."

The doctors did not give Eva food or water. In fact, they wanted her to die. Then they could kill her sister Miriam and perform autopsies to compare the two bodies. Eva was determined not to die. She figured out how to manipulate the thermometer so that doctors would think she was getting better. Finally, she was released from the hospital. When she arrived back at her barracks, she found that Miriam was very ill. Because Eva appeared to be getting better, it was Miriam's turn to be experimented upon.

Racial Hygiene

How could anyone, let alone doctors trained to heal the sick, perform such cruel experiments? Historians point to what was happening in Germany at the time to answer the question.

Like other nations, Germany had overcrowded and dirty slums, where people were desperately poor and diseases spread rapidly. Many Germans blamed these conditions on the "inferior" individuals who lived there, such as criminals and the handicapped and the mentally ill. Those who shared these beliefs about inferior peoples wanted to make it impossible for them to marry and have children. Over time, they reasoned, only Germans with the "best" traits would survive. Their offspring would continue to create a superior human race.

Many German doctors were attracted to this idea of racial hygiene. The doctors viewed the practice as a way to prevent future generations

NAZI EXPERIMENTS

Nazi doctors performed a wide range of horrific experiments on concentration camp inmates during World War II. Here is just a sampling:

- Naked inmates at the Dachau camp in southern Germany were forced to stay outside in freezing temperatures for nine to fourteen hours or were left in freezing cold water. Doctors were trying to simulate the hazards aviators faced when parachuting into the frigid North Sea.

- Doctors placed inmates into an airtight chamber at Dachau and then manipulated the air pressure by reducing and increasing the amount of oxygen. Doctors wanted to see what it was like for aviators to free-fall into space without oxygen or a parachute.

- Doctors at the Natzweiler-Struthof and Sachsenhausen camps in Germany performed a variety of experiments with mustard gas (a chemical that causes damage to the skin, eyes, and body organs). They injected inmates with the gas or forced them to inhale or drink it. They rubbed the gas into wounds. At the Ravensbrück camp for women in northern Germany, broken glass, bacteria, and pieces of wood were also forced into open wounds.

- Doctors at the Buchenwald camp in Germany and also at Dachau and Natzweiler-Struthof experimented with cures for many deadly diseases, including malaria, typhus, and yellow fever.

- Inmates were forced to drink salty seawater at Dachau. Doctors wanted to find out how to make seawater drinkable for shipwrecked sailors or pilots.

- To study how best to kill people, prisoners at Buchenwald were fed poisoned food.

- At Auschwitz, Buchenwald, and Ravensbrück, doctors experimented with techniques to sterilize people, including irritating solutions, chemical injections, surgery, and X-rays.

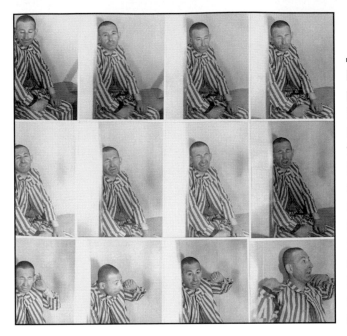

Nazi doctors took photos of this Jewish internee in pressure-chamber experiments to test the human body's reaction to compression and decompression. The doctors documented the man's experience and his later death (by strangulation underwater) in step-by-step photographs.

of Germans from having certain diseases, including social diseases such as criminal behavior. Under German dictator Adolf Hitler, doctors were encouraged to "cure" the "infections" lurking in German society.

The Nazi government enacted laws that legalized racial hygiene. One law ordered that people with genetic disorders, such as blindness, deafness, or physical deformities, be sterilized so they could not have children. Under this law, more than 350,000 Germans were sterilized. By 1939 German doctors were following Hitler's order to put to death mental patients, the handicapped, and others whose lives were not "valuable enough" to continue living.

Jews were also deemed inferior and were forced to live in confined and crowded slums, called ghettos. By 1941 Jews were rounded up off the street and gassed to death inside vans or were shot to death. Trains transported millions of others, like Eva and Miriam, to concentration camps.

With laws and policies already in place to support racial hygiene, German doctors in concentration camps felt free to experiment on the huge number of people there. The Nazis targeted Jews and other groups of prisoners—such as Roma (Gypsies), homosexuals, people with deformities and disabilities, and people of Slavic origin, such as Russians and Poles—for extermination in the camps. Those who disagreed with the government or held other political beliefs, including Communists and Socialists, were also sent to the camps. From the Nazi point of view, these inferior people were perfect subjects for experimentation.

The Nuremberg Code

Germany lost the war in 1945, and the survivors of the concentration camps were freed. The world was horrified by the atrocities in the camps,

EUGENICS IN THE UNITED STATES

The German government adopted racial hygiene as a national policy and enforced it with cruel and extreme measures. But the idea first got its foothold in the United States, when Francis Galton coined the word *eugenics* in 1883. Galton and other eugenicists promoted marriage and reproduction among people with the best traits as a means of improving the human race.

As Jews, Irish, Italians, and other ethnic groups immigrated to the United States in the 1800s and early 1900s, eugenicists feared the country would lose its American identity. They were also concerned that poor people, criminals, and the mentally disabled would overtax the government's financial resources. In 1910 the Eugenics Record Office opened in Cold Spring Harbor, New York. The office housed information on race, heredity, and similar issues. Many prominent people supported eugenics, including U.S. president Theodore Roosevelt and Harvard University president Charles William Eliot.

The Nazis admired the eugenics movement in the United States. Hitler even wrote letters to eugenicists in the United States expressing thanks for books they had written on the topic. The Nazis feared that the United States would climb ahead of the world in establishing a perfect race. In fact, from the 1920s until the 1970s, thirty-two states had sterilization laws. Altogether, about sixty thousand people were sterilized in the United States, including the mentally ill, poor teenagers, young girls who had been raped, people with epilepsy, and those who were considered feebleminded.

In the United States, supporters of eugenics sponsored Better Baby and Fitter Families competitions at state fairs such as this one in Kansas during the first half of the 1900s. Babies and families were judged on physical fitness, personality, and mental qualities. Prizes included medals and champion cups.

and from October 1946 to April 1949, the United States formed a military tribunal, known as the Doctors' Trial, at Nuremberg, Germany. Twenty-three German doctors and health officials stood trial for conspiracy to commit—and for actually committing—war crimes and crimes against humanity. Fifteen were convicted, and seven were found not guilty. An additional physician was convicted of lesser charges. Seven doctors were executed by hanging. The others received prison sentences, some for the

rest of their lives. Mengele—the doctor who had experimented on Eva and Miriam—was immediately arrested after the war ended in 1945. But officials were not aware of his experiments and released him. Mengele eventually fled to South America. While swimming at a resort in Brazil, he had a stroke and died on February 7, 1979.

Because only twenty-three doctors stood trial, it's tempting to think that just a small number of "crazy" doctors committed the crimes. But it

In November 1946, Wilhelm Beiglboeck *(standing, left)* pleaded not guilty to the charges against him at the Doctors' Trial in Nuremberg, Germany. Beiglboeck was a doctor with the Luftwaffe, the German air force. He was found guilty of conducting experiments to test the impact of seawater on humans and was sentenced to a fifteen-year prison sentence. Out of the Doctors' Trial came a groundbreaking code of medical standards governing human medical experimentation.

is important to remember that the entire Nazi health community—all the doctors, nurses, and public health officials—embraced the atrocities. They all shared in the blame.

During the Nuremberg trial, Nazi doctors showed no sorrow or remorse for what they had done. In fact, they defended the inhumane experiments. A chief defense was the war itself. The doctors said that during wartime, considerations of right and wrong could be sacrificed for the good of the country. Harming some people, they reasoned, was okay if it saved the lives of many. In addition, the government was at fault, the doctors said, not individuals. The

doctors were only following orders.

Additional rationales included that the inmates would have died anyway in the camps and that human subjects were actually treated better than other inmates. Experimentation, the doctors said, even offered subjects a chance to "cleanse" themselves. The doctors also claimed that they weren't taught to consider moral and ethical issues. As scientists, they conducted experiments. Others were responsible for deciding what was right and wrong. They further reasoned that the belief that inferiors threatened the health and welfare of Germany required that these people be killed. And they argued that the German experiments were no different from some of the experiments American doctors performed on prisoners.

The most significant outcome of the Doctors' Trial was the establishment of the Nuremberg Code. The trial judges listed ten ethical standards for human subject medical experimentation. The first and most important standard deals with individual consent. The code states that an individual's consent should be voluntary. This means that no one should be forced or coerced to undergo an experiment.

The subject also must be told about the experiment and its risks. The code lists other important requirements, such as experimenting on animals before humans, avoiding mental and physical harm to the subjects, and stopping the experiment if the subject does not want to continue.

The Nuremberg Code became the framework for all future discussion about medical ethics and the laws regarding human subject experimentation. Elie Wiesel, a concentration camp survivor and Nobel Prize-winning human rights advocate, wrote, "[The Nazi killers] knew how to differentiate between good and evil. Their sense of *reality* was impaired. Human beings were not human beings in their eyes. They were abstractions. This is the legacy of the Nuremberg Tribunal and the Nuremberg Code. The respect for human rights in human experimentation demands that we see persons as unique, as ends in themselves."

Eva Mozes Kor and her sister Miriam survived Mengele's experiments. When she grew up, Eva became an advocate for those who were child victims of Nazi experiments. She also opened the CANDLES Holocaust Museum and Education Center in Terre Haute, Indiana, and speaks around the world about medical ethics, forgiveness, and peace. In her personal account, her warning about the perils of human experimentation still rings true: "The scientists of the world must remember that the research is being done for the sake of mankind and not for the sake of science; scientists must never detach themselves from the humans they serve."

Employees at the Y-12 plant at Oak Ridge, Tennessee, change shifts during World War II. The Oak Ridge plant was one of the sites that developed uranium material for nuclear bombs as part of the U.S. government's Manhattan Project. The employees in this photo would have been exposed to radiation in the course of their daily work.

FOR THE GOOD OF MANKIND?

CHAPTER THREE

EXPLOITATION IN THE NAME OF WAR

I was appalled and shocked. It gave me an ache
in my gut and heart.

—U.S. Department of Energy secretary Hazel O'Leary,
condemning U.S. radiation experiments
in the years after World War II, 1993

Ebb Cade, a fifty-five-year-old African American construction worker, was
driving to a job site in Oak Ridge, Tennessee, one morning in March 1945.
He was wedged into the backseat of a car with his two brothers and some
other passengers. On the road ahead, a stalled truck blocked the way. The
driver of Cade's car eased out into the left lane to pass the truck. Suddenly,
a dump truck coming the other way darted into the left lane. The dump
truck sped directly toward Cade's car. Brakes screeched. Tires spun out of
control. The dump truck crashed head-on into Cade's car.

Cade and the other accident victims were rushed to nearby Oak Ridge
Army Hospital. Cade was barely conscious and had fractured his kneecap,
leg, and arm. He was strong and otherwise healthy, so he pulled through
the accident.

What Cade didn't know, though, was that the doctors who cared for him
were part of a secret research study conducted by the Manhattan Project.
The project was a group of U.S. scientists in Los Alamos, New Mexico, who
were working in the 1940s to build an atomic bomb. Doctors in the project
suspected that the radioactive materials they were using were not safe for
humans.

HP-12

At the time of Ebb Cade's car accident in 1945, scientists knew very little about how much radiation humans could tolerate before it would make them sick. In May and August of 1944, several workers at the Los Alamos lab had accidentally been exposed to plutonium. In one instance, plutonium dusted the lab floor. Another time, plutonium leaked from a cracked glass beaker. The radiation contamination levels in the labs began to climb.

Then, on August 1, 1944, a vial of plutonium exploded in the lab. The purple liquid shot onto the wall in front of chemist Don Mastick and bounced back into his mouth. A doctor scrubbed out Mastick's mouth and pumped his stomach, hoping to rid his body of the plutonium. Even after these procedures, his breath alone set off radiation detectors 6 feet (1.8 meters) away.

Researchers panicked. Could the radiation cause a cancer epidemic among the project's workers? If people learned about the dangers of radiation, would the lab workers or people in nearby communities bring lawsuits? If so, the atomic bomb project might be shut down. Many people in the Manhattan Project felt that U.S. national security had to come first. Several key U.S. Army officials, scientists, and doctors decided to secretly test the effects of radiation on the public. Unknown to Cade, he was to be

THE MANHATTAN PROJECT

Just before the start of World War II in 1939, American scientists learned that the Nazis were trying to build an atomic weapon. They feared that if Hitler got his hands on a nuclear bomb, he would wipe out huge numbers of people in Europe and the United States. So, with the support of U.S. president Franklin D. Roosevelt, a secret group of scientists was formed, called the Manhattan Project. Their goal was to construct an atomic bomb. Soon the Manhattan Project had seventy secret research centers spread out across the United States, with its headquarters in Oak Ridge, Tennessee. The main locations were in Chicago, Illinois, and Los Alamos, New Mexico, where the bomb was actually built. U.S. colonel Stafford Warren oversaw the Medical Division of the Manhattan Project, which was assigned the task of experimenting with radiation in humans. By 1942, with U.S. brigadier general Leslie Groves in charge, the Manhattan Project scientists were feverishly racing to produce the first atomic bomb.

the first human injected with one of these dangerous radioactive substances, plutonium-239. Until many years later, Cade would be known by a secret project code name, HP-12. (HP stood for "human product.")

War Is the Answer

How could an innocent car accident victim become an unknowing guinea pig in a dangerous military experiment? The simple one-word answer is *war*. On December 7, 1941, the Japanese had bombed Pearl Harbor in Hawaii, pushing the United States into World War II. The country was immediately thrust into a state of national emergency. The priority became victory over Germany and Japan at all costs.

Suddenly, the U.S. military had to amass huge numbers of troops and develop advanced weapons. Critical national security issues and time pressure diminished the willingness to debate the ethics of human experiments. Decisions to conduct tests on the public, as well as on soldiers, prisoners, and children, were made by just a small group of scientists, military, and government officials. With few laws or guidelines in place and with the urgency of war, the experiments became cloaked in secrecy. It would be decades before the government's dangerous and unethical experimentation was uncovered and exposed.

The U.S. wartime justification for secret human medical experimentation was almost identical to that of the Nazi doctors in the European concentration camps. Unlike the experiments in Germany, though, experiments in the United States were not part of a state-sponsored program to cleanse the population and establish a superior race. However, American doctors frequently abandoned their moral principles to answer questions such as: How effective were U.S. weapons and uniforms? Would new treatments for battlefield wounds and diseases work? How could the troops be protected from attacks by chemical substances such as mustard gas?

First Things First

Before setting Cade's broken bones, the Oak Ridge doctors attended to their experiment. They injected Cade's arm with plutonium—without first obtaining his consent. At the time, scientists had agreed on an amount of plutonium they thought might be safe. But the dosage doctors injected into Cade's arm was much more than that amount. In fact, it was about eighty times more than what most people receive during a year. And the half-life of plutonium-239 (the time it takes for its effects to disappear) is about twenty-four thousand years.

The doctors waited for the radiation to settle into Cade's body. It wasn't until three weeks after the

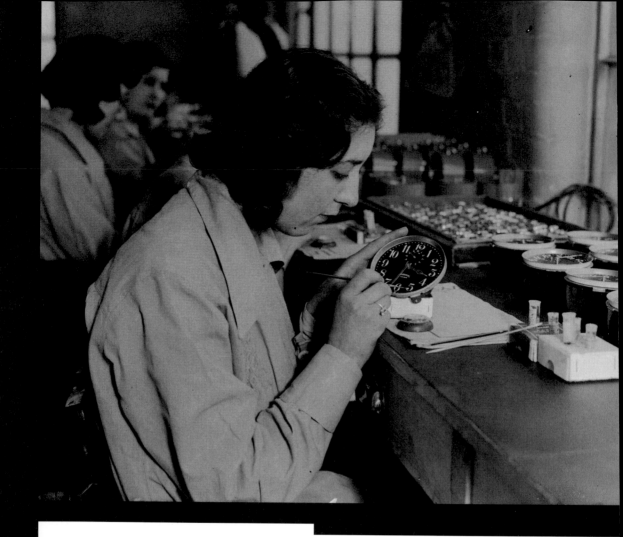

accident that they finally set Cade's broken bones. Even then, the doctors were not yet done with their experiment. While they set Cade's fractures, they also collected bone samples, pulled fifteen of Cade's decayed teeth, and took samples from his jawbone. Everything was analyzed to see how much of the injected radiation Cade's body had absorbed.

Easy Prey

Cade was not the only person injected with plutonium and other radioactive substances. Between April 1945 and July 1947, doctors injected seventeen more people. Purely by chance, all eighteen people had ended up at hospitals where Manhattan Project doctors were looking for human subjects to inject. Although one of the radiation patients apparently signed a consent form, it's not clear how much he was told about the injection he received. The other seventeen patients were completely uninformed.

All the subjects of the radiation experiments were easy prey, in part because patients at this time treated their doctors like gods who could do

WHAT'S A SAFE AMOUNT OF RADIATION?

Manhattan Project scientists learned about the dangers of internal exposure to radiation from the radium dial painters in 1924. Mostly women, these four thousand factory workers illuminated the numbers and hands of watches and other objects with a paint mixture containing small amounts of radium. The workers would often lick the ends of the brushes to get a finer point. Some of the women even used the paint for lipstick or eye makeup. They eventually developed sores in their mouths and on their bodies and couldn't stand without canes. Despite these known dangers, radium was added to candy, face creams, and medicines until about 1932.

After studying the dial painters, Dr. Robley Evans and other scientists concluded that an extremely minute dose of radium in the body might be "safe." But Dr. Robert Stone, the head of the Met Lab's Health Division at the University of Chicago, which was part of the Manhattan Project, wasn't comfortable with relying on a study of so few people. He and other scientists in the project agreed that human experiments were necessary.

In the 1920s, female workers painted the faces of clocks and watches with a black radium-based paint that created a popular shiny look. The paint was highly radioactive and caused radiation poisoning among workers, many of whom developed bone cancer. The use of radium in timekeepers was finally banned in the 1970s.

no wrong. For this reason, it is likely that the radiation patients were too awed by their doctors to question what was going on. In addition, the experiment subjects were not wealthy, powerful individuals who would have had the authority to question or stop the experimentation. Rather, many of the patients were working class, including a handyman, a janitor, a machine shop foreman, and a railroad porter. Five patients were African American. One sixteen-year-old boy, injected with radioactive americium, spoke only Chinese.

Other subjects were desperately ill. For example, cancer patient Una Macke was a very frightened and terminally ill woman. But doctors at Billings Hospital at the University of Chicago in Illinois did not treat her for her illness. Instead, they injected her with a large dose of plutonium—an amount one hundred times more than what scientists believed was safe at the time. She died seventeen days later.

Overall, it is difficult to draw a direct correlation between the radioactive injections and the patients' illnesses and ultimate deaths. Cade's death in 1953 was apparently not related to the injection. On the other hand,

Macke couldn't hold down fluids and food after the injection, so her death may have been accelerated by her reaction to the radiation. Many suffered needlessly. Doctors from UCSF Hospital flew four-year-old Simeon Shaw from Australia (the youngest of the subjects and the only one from a foreign country) for a cancer treatment that he never received. Instead, doctors injected him with radioactive plutonium and performed painful medical tests. He died within a year of his injections.

The cover-up of the radiation injections continued for decades. In 1973 researchers learned that four patients were still alive. Three of them agreed to travel to the University of Rochester's Strong Memorial Hospital in Rochester, New York, for follow-up "study" and "treatment." Instead, more samples were collected. Later that same year, the bodies of those patients who had died were dug up and tested. The word *plutonium* was never mentioned to family members.

Malaria Experiments

Dozens of other wartime human medical experiments took place in the United States during World War II. In 1941 President Franklin D. Roosevelt authorized the establishment of the Committee on Medical Research (CMR), which sponsored countless human subject experiments. One of the CMR's greatest achievements was the development of penicillin, an antibiotic that still saves many lives.

Patriotism ran high in the war years, and across the country, Americans volunteered to participate in medical experiments. In many cases, the volunteers were conscientious objectors, whose religions forbade fighting in combat. Instead of soldiering, objectors were required by law to either serve in the military in noncombat roles or provide alternative service in the United States through the Civilian Public Service. Thousands lived in government-run Civilian Public Service Camps. Many became guinea pigs for a wide range of medical experiments, including exposure to mustard gas, extreme hot and cold temperatures, high altitudes, and starvation diets. Other "volunteers" of wartime experiments were orphans, the mentally ill, the retarded, and prison inmates. As in earlier centuries, many Americans felt it was acceptable to experiment on prisoners and conscientious objectors as a way for these social outsiders to give back to society.

One of the most gruesome wartime experiments was carried out in a prison starting in 1944. At that time, doctors were looking for a cure for malaria, a deadly disease transferred to humans through mosquito bites. As part of their research, doctors allowed malaria-infected mosquitoes to bite prisoners at Stateville Penitentiary in Illinois. The bites caused

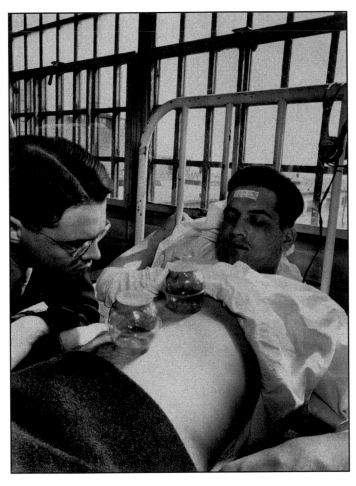

In June 1945, prison inmate Richard Knickerbockers and his doctor in the malaria ward at Stateville Penitentiary in Illinois observe malaria-infected mosquitoes as they bite Knickerbockers's stomach. Many of the volunteers felt they were doing a patriotic service by participating in research to develop antimalarial drugs.

high fevers, vomiting, and fainting. Many prisoners became desperately ill. The Stateville prisoners were also guinea pigs for a variety of malaria treatments that had not been tested before.

Photographers from the popular magazine *Life* snapped photos of the prisoners as they were being bitten. One prisoner, Nathan Leopold, later wrote that the prisoners, happy to do something worthwhile, "took it like men." After the war ended, the governor of Illinois shortened many of the prisoners' jail terms in recognition of their participation in the studies. In addition, the malaria tests became so well known globally that even Nazi doctors in the European concentration camps defended their own tests by citing examples from Stateville.

In fact, until the 1960s, most magazines and newspapers praised the malaria and other wartime "volunteers." In a 1958 article, for example, a *New York Times* reporter wrote, "Among these men and women you will find those who will take shots of the new vaccines, who will swallow radioactive drugs, who will fly higher than anyone else, who will watch malaria-infected mosquitoes feed on their bare arms, who will eat nothing but rice for six weeks and who will permit themselves to be locked alone in chambers too small to stretch their legs."

As for informed consent, the U.S. public was not the least bit worried that the Stateville prisoners may not have given voluntary, informed consent. Instead, they praised their patriotism. The ethics of medical testing on people with limited ability to consent would hardly be questioned again for decades.

Nuclear War!

World War II ended in 1945 after the United States dropped the world's first atomic bombs on Hiroshima and Nagasaki, two cities in Japan, in August of that year. The two bombs obliterated hundreds of thousands of people and their homes, leaving the cities in ruins. Many who survived the bombings died within the next several months from radiation poisoning.

Manhattan Project researchers were afraid that public knowledge of the devastation in Japan would lead to the shutdown of the U.S. bomb-making industry. So officials launched a campaign to downplay the massive injuries, death toll, and environmental hazards. Atomic bombs, they reasoned, were needed to protect Americans. Officials set out to convince the public that atomic bombs could be used safely and that radiation fallout could be controlled.

Cold War Guidelines

Meanwhile, with the end of the war came an increase in the number and type of human radiation experiments. The justification for the ramped-up experiments shifted away from the Manhattan Project to broader concerns for U.S. security. From 1945 to 1991, a period known as the Cold War, the United States feared the growing military and political power of its archenemy, the Communist Soviet Union. U.S. officials began to prepare for the possibility of a Soviet nuclear attack on U.S. soil. Alongside these efforts, researchers continued a wide range of decades-long radiation and bomb-testing experimentation with human subjects.

Yet during the postwar Nuremberg trials, Manhattan Project officials worried that earlier wartime radiation experiments in the United States had been clear violations of the newly established Nuremberg Code. Shortly after the war's end, the Judicial Council of the American Medical Association adopted specific standards. These standards required prior animal testing and voluntary, informed consent for all human medical experimentation.

Then, in 1947, the newly formed U.S. Atomic Energy Commission (AEC)—an organization that regulates the civilian and military development of atomic energy and technology—came up with similar rules. The AEC guidelines required that a human test subject, as well as another family member, both give informed consent for the subject to participate in medical experimentation. Additionally, doctors could not administer harmful substances unless there was reasonable hope that they would help the patient.

Yet even with guidelines in place, researchers routinely and intentionally ignored them. The guidelines were not widely distributed, and researchers tended to make up their own rules about how much radiation they could inflict on unknowing people. Hoping to gain a greater understanding of radiation technology for wartime and medical purposes, the AEC funded thousands of secret human experiments. The army, navy, and air force also funded similar projects.

VANDERBILT STUDY
One of the most horrifying radiation experiments involved 829 pregnant women at a health clinic run by Vanderbilt University Hospital in Tennessee. In the two-year study, which began in 1945, clinic doctors mixed drinks for the women. Doctors told the women that the drinks were good for them and their babies. The drinks, though, were laced with radioactive iron. Many of the mothers who drank the potion and their children lost their hair and teeth. They suffered from blood disorders and broke out in rashes

MANY OF THE MOTHERS WHO DRANK THE POTION (RADIOACTIVE IRON) AND THEIR CHILDREN LOST THEIR HAIR AND TEETH.

and bruises. Some of the women and their children developed cancer and later died.

RADIOACTIVE OATMEAL
A particularly gruesome experiment involved young boys at the Walter E. Fernald State School. This boarding school in Waltham, Massachusetts, was home to mentally deficient and disabled boys as well as boys in trouble with the law or from families too poor to raise them. Researchers from the Massachusetts Institute of Technology wanted to see if certain chemical additives in breakfast cereal deprived the boys of minerals. So from 1946

to 1953, these researchers fed oatmeal laced with radioactive iron and calcium to seventy-four of the school's boys. Fernald's medical director mailed misleading letters to the boys' parents without once mentioning the word *radiation*. The parents were led to believe that the study would "improve the nutrition" of the boys and "help them in general [function] more efficiently than before."

Researchers enticed the unknowing boys to participate in the experiment by promising them membership in a special science club. The boys were happy to join because of popular club outings to the beach and baseball games. In exchange, the boys ate the radioactive cereal, gave the scientists stool and urine samples, and submitted to regular blood tests and X-rays. As adults, many of the Fernald subjects suffered from a host of health issues, which the men were convinced was caused by the experiments.

RADIATION TRACER STUDIES

Thousands of Americans became subjects of so-called radiation tracer studies. The goal of these studies was to trace the spread of radioactive material through the human body. Beginning in 1947, the AEC distributed radioisotopes (elements with unstable nuclei that are radioactive) to hospitals. The AEC hoped the radioactive material would help doctors find cures for cancer. But officials also viewed the studies as an opportunity to impress on the public that radiation could serve beneficial purposes other than bomb building.

In most cases, the radiation doses were small. Some people did get sick from larger amounts. Of greater concern is that most of the subjects did not consent to the radiation or even know they were part of an experiment.

TOTAL BODY IRRADIATION

In other hospital experiments across the country, cancer patients were subjected to a procedure called total body irradiation (TBI). During World War II and then again from 1951 to 1974, doctors administered varied doses of radiation all over the bodies of about seven hundred cancer patients. The patients thought they were undergoing proven and safe treatment for their diseases. But in truth, the doctors were collecting data for the Manhattan Project (later the AEC), the army, navy, air force, and the National Aeronautics Space Administration (NASA). Many patients suffered terrible pain. Others died sooner than anticipated.

Bikini Bombing

Other Cold War experiments sought answers to questions about nuclear war. How would the United States defend against an atomic

OPERATION PAPERCLIP

In 1947 U.S. president Harry Truman signed an executive order expressly forbidding scientists who were active in the Nazi party from entering the United States. But the U.S. State Department and intelligence organizations disobeyed the order. They secretly brought to the United States more than sixteen hundred former Nazi scientists and their families in a program known as Operation Paperclip. The program was named for the paper clips attached to the files of the project's participating scientists.

The Nazi scientists were wanted for their expertise in all kinds of science and technology, including experiments involving the effects of radiation. One Operation Paperclip scientist was involved in TBI experiments. Other scientists studied the effect of the bright flash from atomic blasts on soldiers' eyes. These so-called flash-blindness tests continued for a decade, even after scientists learned that soldiers suffered lasting eye damage and blindness.

blast? Could those in the armed services be protected? What were the effects of radiation on aircraft, tanks, and battleships? Could radiation contamination be reversed or at least contained? Would fear of radiation interfere with the ability of the troops to fight?

One thing was certain—Soviet officials were asking themselves the same questions. As a result, from 1946 to 1992, the U.S. military exploded hundreds of nuclear bombs.

The initial blasts, known as Operation Crossroads, occurred in 1946 at Bikini Atoll (a coral island), about 2,500 miles (4,023 km) southwest of Hawaii. Ninety-five ships (without crew) assembled in the lagoon. Two atomic bombs, together equal in power to the bomb dropped on Nagasaki, targeted the fleet. One, called Able, dropped from a plane. The other, known as Baker, was exploded under the water. The army evacuated the atoll's residents before the blasts, but thousands of U.S. service members stationed at the Pacific blast site received high doses of radiation. In the hopes of salvaging ships that weren't completely destroyed, sailors swabbed the ships' decks and chipped off radioactive paint from the propellers and other equipment. Many were checked later so scientists

At a reception in Washington, D.C., in November 1946, U.S. Navy leadership celebrated the nuclear test bombings of Operation Crossroads. In this image from the party, Vice Admiral William H. P. Blandy and his wife cut into a cake created in the shape of the mushroom cloud that marks the explosion of an atom bomb.

could measure the effects of the doses.

One sailor, seventeen-year-old Dale Beaman, later developed cancer, and his children had related health problems. Another sailor, Harvey Glenn, said, "They checked our clothing, and the [Geiger counter, which tracks radiation levels] was going mad. Then we stuck our bare hands underneath and it did go crazy." Three years later, Glenn was diagnosed with throat cancer.

The military exploded several additional atomic bombs in the Pacific region, decimating animal life, underwater coral reefs, and fish. Radiation levels remained so high that Bikini residents never were able to live on their island again.

TOP SECRET MISTAKE

The TBI experiments, flash-blindness tests, cloud sampling experiments, and others occurred despite a directive by Secretary of Defense Charles E. Wilson on February 23, 1953. Wilson's policy required military and civilian volunteers to sign a consent form before participation in warfare experiments involving chemical, biological, or atomic substances. A witness also was required to sign the form.

In an unfortunate turn of events, the government classified the policy as top secret, probably because of the word *atomic* in the document. As a result, the policy was not widely disseminated. Nor did the policy explain the acceptable level of risk for volunteers in national security experiments. So those who did read the directive were confused about its implementation. Today, Wilson's idea of informed consent is embodied in Army Regulation 70-25, which established a set of protections for subjects in military experiments.

Ground Zero: USA

Despite the known radiation dangers for humans, U.S. officials targeted additional testing sites. But this time, the sites were in the United States. And the justification was the outbreak of the Korean War (1950–1953).

In 1950 President Harry Truman approved recommendations by former Manhattan Project members, as well as the Armed Forces Special Weapons Project (AFSWP), to test bombs at a site near Las Vegas, Nevada. The AEC then set about convincing the public that the tests were safe.

Beginning in 1951, the U.S. government conducted a series of seven atmospheric blasts at the Nevada Test Site. The government also set off other nuclear weapons at the Nevada site, as well as in Alaska, New Mexico, Colorado, and Mississippi. A large underwater bomb was exploded off the coast of San Diego, and three bombs were dropped from rockets above the South Atlantic Ocean.

The government halted atmospheric testing at the Nevada site in 1962. But underground atomic blasts continued until September 1992. In total, the government detonated about 1,030 nuclear weapons.

Huge numbers of U.S. troops—approximately 205,000—participated in the blasts to test the bombs and to see what the effects of radiation would be on humans. For example, during the first test, troops were stationed 7 miles (11 km) away from the detonation site, known as Ground Zero. But in later blasts, they were moved as close as 2 miles (3 km) away. Eventually, a small group of "volunteer" officers agreed to position themselves less than 1 mile (1.6 km) from Ground Zero. Some soldiers were directed to lie in nearby trenches or on the ground while the blasts exploded above. With each detonation, Ground Zero became more contaminated, which exposed troops to even higher levels of radiation.

The U.S. government later claimed that the blasts were military maneuvers designed to test new weapons and to train troops and that actual human experimentation affected only about two thousand to three thousand troops. Officials argued, for example, that tests to measure a pilot's reaction to the bright light from an atomic blast (flash-blindness tests) were actual human experiments. But the "atomic soldiers" have maintained that they all were human guinea pigs in a vast experiment to test the effects of radiation.

In addition to the soldiers at the test sites, U.S. Air Force pilots flew into atomic clouds to find out how far radiation traveled after a blast. The planes had equipment that collected air samples soon after the explosions.

EXPERIMENTING WITH THE AIR WE BREATHE

From 1949 to 1969, the U.S. government conducted more than two hundred secret biological warfare tests in the United States. Officials wanted to be prepared in case of such an attack. As part of the testing, researchers released viruses and bacteria in several states, including Florida, Minnesota, and Missouri, and at the Washington National Airport in Washington, D.C. In June 1966, the Pentagon (the headquarters of the U.S. Department of Defense) dispersed bacteria into the subway tunnels and streets of New York City. A team of investigators secretly sampled the air, surfaces, and people in the area.

Engineers, not doctors, dreamed up the tests. For this reason, the tests were not technically considered human medical experiments. But many people were unintended guinea pigs, and some did get sick.

To measure the effects of inhaled radiation, some pilots flew directly into the blasts as soon as seventeen minutes after the explosion. Some even swallowed water-tight capsules containing photographic film. Later the film was analyzed to measure internal levels of radiation. More than four thousand people were exposed to radiation from flying the planes or from working later with contaminated equipment.

After each blast, doctors checked for radiation exposure. Many troops and pilots later complained of skin disorders such as rashes and blisters. Others lost teeth and hair. Blast veterans also developed cancer. The radiation frequently caused changes to their genes, so their children and grandchildren developed diseases from the inherited genetic mutations.

Downwind and Fallout Dangers

To explore new methods of radiation detection, the AEC approved secret intentional releases of radioactive materials into the air. From 1944 through the 1960s, in a program called the Green Run, officials released these materials from government-owned nuclear sites in Washington State, Utah, Nevada, and Idaho. Releases also occurred in Bayo Canyon, New Mexico, and in the Alaskan wilderness. In addition, many releases occurred accidentally. For example, leaks from the Hanford plutonium-manufacturing complex in Washington State outnumbered all the intentional releases from the Green Run.

Researchers tested the surrounding downwind areas for radiation contamination. At Hanford, for example, scientists visited the local schools to monitor the levels of the radiation on farm children, who drank the milk from the region's contaminated cows and ate radiated food grown on the farms. While waiting a turn to climb inside machines to be measured for radiation, the children read comic books given to them by the researchers.

Americans across the country developed a range of health issues, such as cancers, allergies, and birth defects in their children. A National Cancer Institute (NCI) study in 1997 stated that radiation released at the Nevada site may cause between ten thousand and seventy-five thousand extra cases of thyroid cancer. At the time, the NCI estimated that about 70 percent had yet to be diagnosed.

Most radioactive particles (called fallout) disperse in the vicinity of an atomic explosion. But if the explosion is aboveground, wind can blow the fallout hundreds of miles away. Smaller particles can travel into the stratosphere, between 5 to 31 miles (8 to 50 km) above Earth, depending on the latitude. These particles are swept up in global currents and can travel around the world.

Researchers feared that atomic tests would be halted unless the public's

Hazel O'Leary, U.S. secretary of energy from 1993 to 1997, chose to declassify documents from the Cold War era proving that the U.S. government had used U.S. citizens—without their consent—in human radiation experiments.

fear of global fallout could be alleviated. Beginning in 1953, U.S. scientists secretly started collecting corpses to check for radiation exposure. This practice continued through the 1980s. In one project, called Operation Sunshine, U.S. government researchers examined body parts from about fifteen thousand corpses from around the world. Family members were not consulted and did not give their consent.

Exposing the Cover-Up

Forty-six years after the last secret experimental patient was injected with plutonium, Eileen Welsome, a reporter for the *Albuquerque Tribune,* uncovered their names and stories. Through Welsome's

newspaper articles in 1993, the experiments came to the attention of Hazel O'Leary, the head of the U.S. Department of Energy.

O'Leary was appalled to learn that the government had secretly

"WHAT I'VE READ LEADS ME TO BELIEVE THAT BY THE STANDARDS OF TODAY, INFORMED CONSENT COULD NOT HAVE TAKEN PLACE."—HAZEL O'LEARY, HEAD OF THE U.S. DEPARTMENT OF ENERGY, 1993

violated the trust of Americans and put them at risk of serious injury. As she spoke at a news conference in 1993, an overhead projector highlighted the words of an important new Department of Energy policy: "The Cold War is over…we're coming clean." "What I've read," she said about the plutonium injections, "leads me to believe that by the standards of today, informed consent could not have taken place."

The information led President Bill Clinton to form the Advisory Committee on Human Radiation Experiments (ACHRE) to investigate the thousands of radiation experiments conducted in the United States after World War II. ACHRE recommended compensation to very few people but did name the families of those injected with plutonium, as well as fourteen people subjected to TBI experiments. In a less strongly worded recommendation, ACHRE suggested compensating those injured from experiments that had no therapeutic value. The committee further proposed that the government apologize to the unharmed victims who did not give voluntary consent. But the committee did not blame specific doctors or any particular government agency. And regardless of the known dangers of radiation, it did not advise prohibiting future intentional releases of radiation.

Finally, on October 3, 1995, the U.S. government publicly acknowledged the wrongs committed against the atomic veterans and all the radiation victims and their families, as well as to their communities. In a public apology, President Bill Clinton spoke about the experiments. He noted that "some were unethical, not only by today's standards, but by the standards of the time in which they were conducted. They failed both the test of our national values and the test of humanity." The experiments harmed "those citizens who count most on the government for its help, the destitute and the gravely ill…[and] members of the military, precisely those on whom we and our government count most."

A year later, O'Leary met in Rochester, New York, with some of the families of those injected with plutonium. In attendance were the relatives of HP-1, HP-4, HP-5, HP-6, HP-8, and HP-9. Her comments after the meeting echoed the sadness and disillusionment felt by many of the relatives. "My commitment is: Never Again," she said. "This should never happen again in government."

As part of U.S. Army experiments into chemical warfare, prisoners were often unknowing participants. In this image, medical administrator Solomon McBride *(in lab coat)* talks with a subject of one of the experiments at Holmesburg Prison in Pennsylvania in 1966. Note the patches on the prisoner's back, where chemicals were applied to the skin.

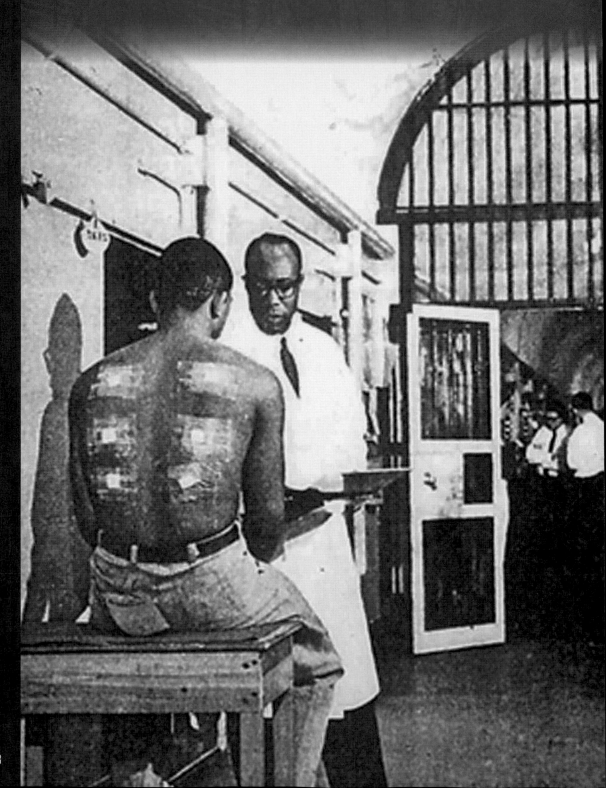

CHAPTER FOUR

SHIFTING ATTITUDES IN THE WAKE OF SCANDAL

It was a good code for barbarians but an unnecessary code
for ordinary physician-scientists.

—Jay Katz, Yale Law School ethicist,
explaining the U.S. medical community's dismissal of the Nuremberg Code, 1992

Al Zabala, an inmate at Holmesburg Prison in Philadelphia, Pennsylvania, doesn't remember most of what happened when he was injected with a dangerous mind-altering drug. He only knows that for a week in 1964, doctors observed him through a peep slot in a padded room. But Zabala does remember how he felt later: "I wasn't right for a month after the test. I was real subdued and quiet.... They put me on a liquid diet until I could swallow whole food again. When we finally came back to the population, all the guys in the study had to wear badges that said we were not responsible for our actions."

Zabala was one of the lucky "volunteers." Other inmates "didn't remember their names. Guys would fade in and out of consciousness.... Some guys beat themselves up...they had violent, ugly [drug-induced] trips—dogs as big as horses, worms like alligators—horrible trips, being eaten by giant spiders.... One guy said he was hung and killed."

Testing Chemical Weapons

Zabala and other inmates were unknowing players in U.S. Army experiments with chemical weapons. The army wanted to develop chemical agents that could affect an enemy's performance on the battlefield but not permanently injure or kill him. From 1955 to 1975, about eight thousand members of the armed forces, prisoners, and civilians participated in the experiments. In Zabala's case, doctors probably administered lysergic acid diethylamide (LSD), a drug that creates hallucinations. Several years later, Zabala began to black out, sometimes for days, without any memory of what had happened.

The army conducted the tests in three trailers set up in the Holmesburg courtyard. In 1971 the Central Intelligence Agency (CIA) came on board and secretly experimented on prisoners with truth serums and other mind-control drugs.

Over the years, the Holmesburg inmates gave many reasons for volunteering in the experiments. Some did so for patriotic reasons, while others said they volunteered "for science." Most of them, though, participated for money. The payment was small, but it was more than what they received for other prison jobs. Experiments also relieved the boredom of daily life in prison. Some inmates undoubtedly hoped their prison terms might be shortened or that they might receive better food or other privileges. The inmates trusted the doctors and thought they wouldn't be hurt.

Prison guards didn't complain about the experiments either. They were happy the experiments kept the inmates busy and easy to guard. For the doctors, using inmates meant the experiments were inexpensive to run. For example, many prisoners were taught to run the experiments, so administrative costs were low. In addition, the experiments could be conducted over a period of time, with the same subjects, to provide consistent results. Plus, diet and other test conditions could be controlled for the same reason. Most inmates were poor, uneducated, and African American—a group that asked few probing questions. This "conspiracy of silence" among the inmates, guards, and doctors kept the experiments operating for years without exposure to the media or the general public.

THIS "CONSPIRACY OF SILENCE" AMONG THE INMATES, GUARDS, AND DOCTORS KEPT THE PRISON EXPERIMENTS OPERATING FOR YEARS WITHOUT EXPOSURE TO THE MEDIA OR THE GENERAL PUBLIC.

Universities Join In

The military and the CIA were not the only ones taking advantage of prisoners for medical research. Universities and drug companies also funded studies. Up until the early 1970s, drug companies used prisoners around the country for 90 percent of their studies.

From 1954 to 1974, for example, the University of Pennsylvania ran a research lab at Holmesburg headed by Dr. Albert Kligman, a renowned university dermatologist. Excited by the prospects of unlimited prisoner experimentation for a variety of skin disorders, Kligman said in an interview, "All I saw before me were acres of skin. It was like a farmer seeing a fertile field for the first time."

One inmate, Johnnie Williams, reported how Kligman and his team burned his skin with "sulfuric acid and carbolic acid" and a "microwave light." For an hour every day one month, they soaked his arms in harsh chemicals. His skin thickened "like leather." Doctors also cut into his armpits to examine his sweat glands. Doctors experimenting with sutures sewed Williams's skin with stitches "to see if they would dissolve." Doctors also slashed his back to purposely induce overgrown scars called keloids. Williams was even injected with skin from a corpse "to see if it would grow."

In one of the most toxic experiments, Kligman swabbed the inmates' backs with a chemical called dioxin. The Holmesburg inmates were particularly concerned because veterans of the Vietnam War (1957–1975) who had been exposed to dioxin later developed skin sores, cancer, and genetic deformities.

Exposed!

These medical studies, as with many others in the United States after World War II, ignored the Nuremberg Code in all areas of human subject experimentation, and not just with prisoners. Confined and convenient people routinely became guinea pigs for the purpose of human medical experimentation. U.S. doctors felt that "no code drawn up in response to [Nazi doctors] was relevant to the United States."

All U.S. doctors, though, did not quietly follow the pack. In 1966 Dr. Henry Beecher, a Harvard medical school professor, published an article in the *New England Journal of Medicine.* Beecher was not a staunch supporter of the code. He thought that ethical and knowledgeable doctors could be trusted without rules that tied their hands. Even so, he shook the foundations of research on humans by openly exposing about twenty-two instances of unethical experiments where informed consent was questionable or not obtained. He discovered the examples simply by reading research already widely published in medical journals. Beecher alerted the press and television stations about his article's imminent publication, which heightened the scandals. The public was outraged.

Willowbrook Experiments

In one experiment from the 1950s through the 1970s, for example, Dr. Saul Krugman injected hepatitis into developmentally delayed children at Willowbrook State School in Staten Island, New York. At that time, hepatitis (a virus that attacks the liver) was rampant among confined, institutionalized people. Krugman and his research team wanted to find a way to prevent the disease from developing and spreading.

Willowbrook was overcrowded, and new applicants were denied admission. Yet doctors at the school allowed new children to be admitted into a special research ward if the parents agreed to their children's participation in the hepatitis studies. A letter to the parents explained that some children would be intentionally infected with hepatitis, but it did not provide information about the hazards of the disease.

The doctors' research confirmed earlier studies that injections of gamma globulin (blood containing antibodies) could boost the immune system and prevent hepatitis A. But the discovery was buried in Beecher's condemnation of the ethical violations.

Americans wondered whether research should be conducted on people whose intellectual limitations made them incapable of giving informed consent. Also, were parents making truly informed choices on behalf of their children? Did they feel pressured to agree to the research, knowing that they had few available schools for their disabled children? Did the doctors put unfair pressure on the parents by threatening to deny a place in the school unless they agreed to the research?

The doctors argued that the harm was minimal. They felt the children probably would have contracted the disease eventually since Willowbrook was plagued with hepatitis. Plus, they pointed out that by catching the disease, the children developed immunities to protect against future outbreaks. Some critics compared this end-justifies-the-means argument to the Nazi defenses during the Nuremberg trial.

Jewish Chronic Disease Hospital Study

Beecher also discussed a scandalous experiment involving Dr. Chester Southam at the Jewish Chronic Disease Hospital in Brooklyn, New York, in 1963. Southam was a well-respected specialist in the study of viruses. He thought that a virus caused cancer and was concerned that scientists conducting cancer research might catch the disease.

Southam first tested this idea in 1954 at Sloan-Kettering Institute for Cancer Research in New York City. He injected cancer patients with cancer cells from other people. Then two years later, he moved on to inject healthy people with cancer cells. This time, the subjects were prisoners at the

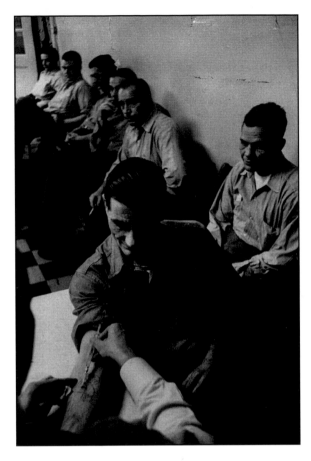

Doctors at Ohio State Penitentiary injected live cancer cells into prisoners as part of Dr. Chester Southam's ten-year study of human immunity to cancer. Southam was convinced that cancer could be cured through vaccination, though the subjects of his experiments were not told the truth about the substance of the injections.

Ohio State Penitentiary. Over the years, Southam injected more than six hundred people. He did not tell any of the subjects about the contents of the injections. Many grew tumors.

Three doctors at the Jewish Chronic Disease Hospital refused to inject cancer cells into twenty-two elderly patients without first getting their consent. They based their refusal on the Nuremberg Code. When another doctor at the hospital injected the patients anyway, the three doctors resigned.

The media got wind of the case. When asked by an interviewer why he hadn't injected himself with the cancer cells, Southam said, "There are relatively few skilled cancer researchers, and it seemed stupid to take even the little risk."

The National Institute of Health (NIH) decided to investigate the Brooklyn hospital case and other experiments funded by the NIH. In 1966, for the first time, the NIH concluded that committees must review and approve human subject experiments before granting federal funds. The committees would be comprised of researchers, as well as a diverse group

THALIDOMIDE BABIES

The outrage over Dr. Chester Southam's injections was partly due to the public's heightened awareness of medical tragedy in the thalidomide scandal from the year before. In 1962 U.S. newspapers were flooded with accounts of birth defects in Europe linked to thousands of pregnant women taking thalidomide, a drug for morning sickness. Photos of children with flipperlike arms and legs shocked the public. Since Dr. Frances Oldham Kelsey had successfully prevented the U.S. Food and Drug Administration (FDA) from approving the drug in the United States, U.S. thalidomide birth deformities were rare. The thalidomide cases did not arise from human experimentation, yet in the eyes of the public, Southam's unethical behavior was another reminder of how medicine could go terribly awry.

of people from different ethnic, class, and racial backgrounds.

The NIH rules marked the beginning of a change—now a committee, as opposed to just an individual doctor, would review patient consent. Beecher's article had led to heightened public awareness of the dangers of uninformed medical experimentation. Yet even with this knowledge and the new NIH rules, more scandal came to light in the 1970s.

The Tuskegee Syphilis Study

In 1932 officials at the U.S. Public Health Service (PHS) devised a research experiment to study syphilis among African American men. Syphilis is a sexually transmitted disease. If left untreated, the disease can cause heart problems; blindness; insanity; and, finally, death.

At the time, syphilis plagued many poor black men who lived in Macon County, Alabama. Dr. Taliaferro Clark, an official at PHS, suggested that instead of spending money for the costly treatment of so many people, the government should observe the progression of the disease to learn more about its stages. So began the Tuskegee Syphilis Study.

The PHS doctors organized a free health day for the community to identify men for the study. Poor black people, who could not afford health care, flocked to the clinic to get their blood drawn. They were led to believe they would receive safe medical tests and free treatments for any illness discovered.

The doctors identified and enrolled in their study 399 black farmers who were in the late stages of syphilis. They also formed a control group of 201 healthy men. (Control groups allow researchers to compare results among healthy and sick individuals in a study.) Neither the healthy nor the sick men were told they were subjects of a federal government experiment. They thought the nearby Tuskegee Institute (a university for African Americans) and the local health department were treating them for "bad blood."

The PHS followed the men until 1972. When doctors realized in the 1940s that penicillin could cure syphilis, the men were never offered the medicine. Instead, to keep up the pretense of offering treatment, the PHS provided physical exams, aspirins, and vitamins. The men also were convinced to stay in the study by offers of free lunches and free funerals.

In this undated photo, a doctor draws blood from a subject of the Tuskegee Syphilis Study. As part of a settlement with participants and their families in the 1970s, the U.S. government promised lifetime medical and health benefits and burial services to all living participants and their immediate family (wives and offspring). The last study participant died in January 2004.

Although the Tuskegee study wasn't widely discussed, it wasn't secret either. Published articles reported the results from autopsies of the men who died. Yet knowledgeable doctors, nurses, and government officials didn't question the ethics of watching black men sicken and die horrible deaths.

Then in the 1960s, the civil rights movement burst into the public conscience with increasing intensity. To fight racial oppression, black people and their supporters staged sit-ins and protest marches. The anger over racial inequality was so great that race riots erupted in large urban areas across the country. National Guard troops fended off angry white crowds who refused to let black children attend white schools in the South. In this climate, Peter Buxton, a worker at PHS, learned about the Tuskegee study in 1965. He confronted officials to stop the study. Despite heightened sensitivity to discrimination against black people, no one listened. For seven years, even after he left PHS, Buxton periodically wrote letters to the service. Finally, out of frustration, Buxton told the story to a journalist.

On July 25, 1972, the Tuskegee story hit the newsstands. Americans were shocked. Outrage over the lack of ethics in the Tuskegee study, combined with the social and political climate of the day, created a powerful force for change.

OUTRAGE OVER THE LACK OF ETHICS... CREATED A POWERFUL FORCE FOR CHANGE.

The National Research Act

In the wake of the Tuskegee scandal, U.S. senator Edward Kennedy of Massachusetts chaired congressional hearings about experiments on prisoners and other vulnerable human test subjects. As a result of the hearings, Congress passed the National Research Act in 1974. The act created a federal commission called the National Commission for the Protection of Human Subjects of Biomedical and Behavioral Research (CPBBR). The commission's goal was to "identify the basic ethical principles" underlying human subject experimentation and "to develop guidelines" to assure that those principles would be followed.

In response to the congressional hearings and heightened public criticism of the prisoner experiments, on March 1, 1976, the director of the Bureau of Prisons, Norman A. Carlson, declared an end to medical experimentation on federal prisoners. Soon state prisons followed his lead. Most prisoner experiments halted within about four years.

But the prohibiting of prison experimentation did not last. The commission backtracked from Carlson's ban, mostly because the inmates themselves complained, as did the FDA. Although the experiments were often harsh, the inmates wanted the money they could earn, an amount that was greater than what they received from other prison jobs. They also enjoyed the benefits of health care and the relative safety and freedom experienced in the laboratory settings.

AFTER DECADES OF UNETHICAL TESTING, RESEARCHERS WERE FINALLY FORCED TO FOLLOW THE PRINCIPLES OF THE NUREMBERG CODE.

The Department of Health, Education, and Welfare (later the Department of Health and Human Services) developed a stringent set of guidelines for prison experimentation, which the commission and the FDA endorsed. The guidelines allow prisoners to be used for therapeutic research involving minimal risk.

The commission's final report in 1979, called the Belmont Report, revolutionized the field of human subject experimentation. After decades of unethical testing, researchers were finally forced to follow the principles of the Nuremberg Code. Three ethical principles—respect for persons, beneficence, and justice—are the hallmarks of the report.

The principle of respect requires that all human subjects give voluntary and informed consent. Beneficence refers to maximizing the subject's benefits from the experiment and limiting harm. For experiments to be just, everybody, not just one group of people, must benefit from the research. In addition, a range of people must bear the burden of testing new treatments, not just the poor and uneducated. This means that subjects must represent a diverse group, crossing the boundaries of race, economic class, age, and ethnic backgrounds.

The Common Rule

These three principles became the framework for federal laws that were adopted in 1981 to guide human medical experimentation. Known as the Common Rule, these laws also regulate research on vulnerable people, such as the mentally ill and children. The FDA adopted similar regulations for the testing and approval of new drugs, medical devices, and biologics (products produced from biological substances, such as vaccines) for sale.

The commission wrestled with how to provide needed care in situations where people could not always speak for themselves and where research was needed for the good of society. The law provides different categories of risk and specifies when consent from parent and child is mandated. In most cases, regardless of the level of risk, a parent must give informed consent and children who are old enough to understand must consent as well. The law remains unclear as to when an authorized person can volunteer a mentally disabled person in a study.

One of the most important elements of the Common Rule was the creation of Institutional Review Boards (IRBs). These boards review all federally funded human subject experiments and have the power to approve or reject them. The IRB's job is to make sure that experiments comply with the Common Rule.

Yet, despite the enactment of laws protecting human subjects, many problems still exist and people continue to get hurt. Some studies remain unethical, and laws are violated. Other experiments point out a recurring dilemma: people are needed in medical trials that may ultimately harm them.

In the twenty-first century, millions of Americans participate in research trials across the country. Future medical advancements, particularly in the area of genetics, hold great promise for cures to serious medical conditions. How can we strike a balance between the individual rights of the participant and society's demand for medical advancement?

CHAPTER FIVE

CAN WE SAFEGUARD HUMAN RISKS?

When we teach, we must not see any person as an abstraction.

Instead, we must see in every person a universe

with its own secrets, with its own treasures,

with its own sources of anguish,

and with some measure of triumph.

Eli Wiesel, Nazi concentration camp survivor and human rights advocate, 1992

When Jesse Gelsinger was almost three years old, he fell asleep in front of the television. His parents couldn't wake him up. They rushed him to the hospital. It turned out that Jesse had a genetic disorder that caused a rare disease known as OTC (ornithine transcarbamylase deficiency).

Jesse was missing a gene that helps break down ammonia in the body. Some children die from this condition, but Jesse's case was manageable with medication. Even so, as he grew up, he was in and out of hospitals for emergency treatment, had to swallow more than fifty pills a day, and was forced to stick to a strict diet.

When he turned eighteen, Jesse decided to enroll in a gene transfer study at the University of Pennsylvania in Philadelphia. Dr. James Wilson and his team had created a special virus that carried a good copy of Jesse's missing gene. The doctors wanted to inject Jesse with the virus to learn how much of the virus could be tolerated before serious side effects set in.

Jesse understood that the injection was not a treatment. He knew that he personally would not benefit from the gene therapy. But he wanted to help find a cure for young children with more serious forms of OTC. Jesse and his family trusted the doctors, who had assured them that the experiment was safe. The doctors injected Jesse with a high dose of the virus on September 13, 1999. Within hours, he became dangerously ill. As Jesse's conditions worsened, his doctors did not put a stop to the trial, and just four days after the injection, Jesse died.

As eventually became clear, Jesse's doctors did not follow the study protocol approved by the FDA. The doctors injected the virus despite the fact that Jesse's ammonia levels exceeded the authorized amount. The protocol itself was poorly designed. Doctors usually conduct high-risk trials only on seriously ill patients. But Jesse was exposed to a dangerous health risk at a time when his illness was relatively stable and manageable.

In addition, neither the consent form nor Jesse's doctors clarified for him and his family the harmful, even deadly, side effects the doctors knew about from earlier testing of the virus on both monkeys and people. In fact, researchers had purposely—and illegally—withheld the results of adverse reactions from federal regulators and the IRBs. Later, Jesse's father learned of another serious ethical breach. Dr. Wilson owned a 30 percent interest in the company that was planning to develop and sell the treatment based on the results of the experiment on Jesse and others. The University of Pennsylvania also owned stock in the company.

The Business of Medical Research

Jesse's experience shined a spotlight on the exploding business of medical research. The prospect of huge financial gains from new medical drugs and other treatments has fueled an atmosphere of intense competition and pressure to find results quickly. This in turn can compromise the safety of human subjects.

Each year, researchers test more and more new drugs and other treatments in research studies called clinical trials. The number of human subjects required for these trials has skyrocketed. For example, one company that enrolled volunteers estimated that from 1999 to 2005, the number of people needed for clinical trials worldwide jumped from 2.8 million to 19.8 million.

Human subjects are protected much more than they were years ago. Huge medical advancements have been achieved, and as a rule, clinical trials are safer than in years past. The Common Rule, though, has not kept up with the medical research boom.

When the federal laws were first enacted in 1981, researchers at universities and medical schools conducted most of the medical research. The academic approach focused on learning, teaching, and serving the public good. Human participants often volunteered to participate in experimental studies to help solve important research questions. The federal government and nonprofit organizations, such as those that fight cancer and heart disease, funded most experiments.

In the twenty-first century, however, drug-manufacturing companies pay for many of the studies, including those conducted at academic institutions. Tremendous financial rewards propel the clinical trials, as companies strive to discover the next best-selling drug. Profits from new drugs can be in the billions of dollars.

Speed means profit. Once a company obtains a patent for a particular drug, other companies are legally prohibited from making and selling that same drug for twenty years. It can take a company a decade or longer to research, test, and gain FDA approval for a new drug, at a cost of millions of dollars. For that reason, drug-manufacturing companies continue to work on their own versions of patented drugs so they can obtain FDA approval as early as possible during any twenty-year period. In this way, as patents expire, companies are ready to immediately launch replacement drugs they hope will be blockbusters.

Yet often, researchers cut corners or overstate testing results. They may fear funding cuts from sponsors if results are poor. Or perhaps a prestigious teaching position at a university hinges on the achievement of new medical knowledge. And because academic institutions are unequipped to conduct research quickly, the vast majority of drug trials are farmed out to yet another business—contract research organizations (CROs). The CROs manage and guide each clinical trial from enrollment of the participants to FDA approval.

IRBs for Hire

When multiple clinical trials for one drug are conducted around the country, federal law mandates that an IRB—of which there are thousands in the United States—must review and okay each one before FDA approval. If one IRB refuses permission, the trial can still go forward as long as another IRB grants its seal of approval. Essentially, CROs can shop around until they get authorization. A further complication arises when members of an IRB are biased in favor of researchers they know or on behalf of an institution, such as a university, that employs them. In these cases, authorization may be granted because of personal connections and not because of the strength of the trial itself.

Most IRBs are for-profit businesses. Companies or sponsors of the trial pay the boards for their services. The more reviews an IRB conducts, the more money it makes. And an IRB that provides speedy approval gets lots of business.

Technically, the federal government's Office for Human Research Protections (OHRP) and the FDA provide oversight for clinical studies. However, the large number of trials makes enforcement difficult. The Department of Health and Human Services issued a report in 2007 stating that the FDA had only two hundred inspectors to check about 350,000 test sites. In addition, only about 1 percent of all drug trials were audited, and most on-site checks are performed to verify data collection rather than to look for safety violations.

IRBs share in the responsibility of oversight, but this usually means only reviewing documents, such as consent forms, to evaluate safety. They usually don't go to the trial sites themselves or ask sponsors difficult questions. In one notorious case in Miami, Florida, in 2006, officials shut down a 675-bed experimentation site because of serious fire and safety hazards as well as ethical violations. Many of the trial participants were undocumented immigrants who didn't speak English well and therefore did not fully understand the dangers of the experiments.

Show Me the Data

Currently, federal laws only protect people in studies that receive federal funds. Many institutions, such as colleges and universities, follow the Common Rule anyway. Technically, they don't have to, however, unless the federal government pays for the particular study. In these situations, oversight may be minimal.

This points to an additional oversight problem—the lack of statistical data. A central data collection system does not yet exist. For this reason, the numbers of injuries to participants, poor results, and other problems that occur during research often remain unknown.

Is Volunteering Voluntary?

With laws limiting the use of prisoners and other vulnerable populations for medical experimentation, volunteers mostly come from the general public. Many important ethical questions continue to surround the issue of voluntary participation, however. How should volunteers be recruited? Are the risks too high for healthy volunteers in Phase I clinical trials? Should only seriously ill people be enrolled? How can consent forms be changed so that volunteers fully understand all the risks? Can children and people with mental deficiencies authorize consent?

A major problem lies in the nature of research studies themselves. Experimental research is just that—an experiment. As bioethicist Jerry Menikoff explains, "In most instances, the study is *not* being conducted

CLINICAL TRIALS

Some clinical trials test new treatments, such as drugs, surgery, and medical devices. Others aim at prevention, such as vaccines. The first stage of testing, called Phase I, has the potential to be the most dangerous. At this stage, a small number of healthy people are the first to test a new drug or treatment. Phase I subjects are usually paid to participate. In some Phase I trials for diseases such as cancer or AIDS, volunteers are patients who may be very ill. Phase I trials test safety, discover side effects, and learn how the body reacts.

In Phase II trials, hundreds of patients with a specific medical problem enroll to test a new treatment for their condition. Researchers monitor safety and begin to see if the treatment works. In Phase III trials, thousands of patients with the specific disease participate in studies that are usually randomized. This means that some subjects are randomly chosen to receive the standard treatment on the market, while others receive the new medication. The effectiveness of the two is then compared.

In some randomized trials, another group is assigned a placebo. Placebos are pills that have no medical effect at all. In many instances, people get better when they are given a pill, even if it is made of sugar. This is known as the placebo effect and is attributed to the fact that people believe they are receiving treatment. Placebos are not used when a participant's health would be seriously compromised by not receiving the standard care.

Many clinical trials are "healthy people studies." These usually take place in hospital settings, where healthy volunteers participate in minimally invasive procedures such as a new screening test or a specific use for an MRI scan.

primarily to treat (or 'do good things for'…) the people who participate as subjects in the study." The purpose of a clinical trial is only to advance medical understanding of a particular question. Patients may end up benefiting from the research or new drug, but that is not the goal.

In addition, doctors and researchers have different duties of care under the law. This distinction holds true even when a researcher happens to be a doctor or even a subject's personal physician. In a doctor-patient relationship, a doctor must provide care that is in the best interests of the patient.

But the legal duty of care between a researcher (or a doctor acting as a researcher) and a test subject is not nearly as high. The Common Rule merely states that the risks to a subject must be reasonable in relationship to the benefits to the subject and to society's benefit from acquiring new knowledge. The benefits to the test subject don't need to outweigh the risks. In other words, an experiment that the IRB views as worthy of approval may not actually have positive benefits for the subject.

"Just a Simple Thing"

It's easy to see how a participant might think that a clinical trial will help her, particularly in cases such as Jolee Mohr's. In Mohr's situation, her own doctor recruited her and other volunteers and conducted the research. Mohr had rheumatoid arthritis, a condition that causes painful swelling of the joints. Aside from the arthritis, though, Mohr was a healthy, thirty-six-year-old woman with a husband and a young daughter.

WHAT'S A GOOD STUDY FOR A VOLUNTEER?

Are you willing to expose yourself to risk when you may not gain a personal benefit? Before making a decision, it is important to know that doctors can prescribe cutting-edge treatments or drugs, which may mean there is no need to enroll in a trial. This is particularly true with cancer treatments such as chemotherapy. Also, once the FDA approves a drug, doctors can prescribe it for a variety of purposes, not just the ones listed on the bottle's label.

Most new drugs are modified slightly to replace drugs with expired patents. So someone with a medical condition may opt for the standard treatment that works rather than try a modified version that hasn't been widely tested. If a trial is randomized, so that some subjects receive the new treatment and some receive the standard care, a subject may only have a 50 percent chance of receiving the new treatment. If a person is hoping to get the experimental treatment, she may decide not to enroll in the trial.

Jolee Mohr (with her husband and their daughter in a photo from 2006) died from massive bleeding and organ failure just three weeks after experimental gene-therapy treatment for rheumatoid arthritis. Deep within the 15-page consent form she signed was a statement clarifying that doctors did not actually anticipate any "direct medical benefits from participation in this study."

Mohr's doctor was conducting a clinical trial of a new gene therapy. Unbeknownst to Mohr, the company sponsoring the trial paid the doctor for each subject he recruited. Although most of Mohr's symptoms were relieved with medication, her doctor suggested that she join the trial. He injected Mohr's knee with the drug therapy in his office. On July 24, 2007, just three weeks after the injection, Mohr was dead.

It's unclear what actually caused Mohr's death. Of concern, though, is that Mohr did not understand the risks of the trial nor of her doctor's financial arrangement with the sponsoring company. Mohr's husband told one reporter, "It was presented to her like this is going to make her knee better. It was supposed to be just a simple thing."

After an investigation, the FDA allowed the clinical trial to proceed despite Mohr's death. But her death raised issues of informed consent and a doctor's conflicts of interest similar to those in Jesse Gelsinger's case eight years earlier. If Mohr had known about the risks and of her doctor's financial arrangement with the drug company, would she have gone ahead with the trial? We'll never know.

Motivation to Risk All

We do know from research studies, though, that the more information a person receives about a trial, the less likely it is that the person will choose to enroll. Yet, in a typical Phase I cancer study, where the drugs tested can be extremely dangerous and the risks of harm are exceptionally high, subjects appear overly optimistic that they will benefit from the study. What's going on? Why would people agree to participate in such dangerous studies?

In general, people who are desperate for a cure to their illness want to believe there is hope. They also tend to believe that they will be the lucky ones to benefit from experimental trials. Others participate simply because the consent forms are vague and the full scope of risks is not laid out clearly.

With the Common Rule and FDA regulations in place, informed consent is much better than it was years ago. The question, though, is how much better? In the past, researchers frequently revealed very little information to subjects or none at all. With consent now mandated by law, the problem is that the risks are not conveyed clearly enough.

In addition, the current consent rules do not protect unsophisticated patients who may not question the risks and benefits from a particular trial.

Some researchers worry that fewer people will volunteer if they are given more information. And fewer study participants may result in less medical advancement.

Is Money the Answer?

Some people feel that one way to encourage enrollment in experimental studies, yet more fairly distribute the burden, is for sponsors or researchers to pay participants money. FDA regulations specifically state that money may be offered to recruit subjects but only in amounts that would not be considered coercion. The FDA leaves it to the IRBs to set rates and amounts of payment. To avoid coercing subjects to participate, IRBs typically try to keep payments low—close to the minimum wage.

Payment of subjects is very controversial. Some regulators worry that payments lead people to engage in dangerous risks that they would otherwise not agree to. This is particularly true in Phase I studies, where healthy participants may be paid to test a new and potentially toxic drug. Unlike decades ago, most healthy people no longer volunteer just to help medical science, unless the study is for a procedure that involves minimal risk. Phase I drug volunteers typically are poor, unemployed, former prisoners, or students. These people usually participate for one reason: money.

People in need of money might be unlikely or unwilling to closely evaluate a study's risks. Paradoxically, they may not be able to afford to buy the new treatments if they prove successful. They assume the burden of experimental testing for society but may not be able to gain any benefits from the new research.

Also, most of these participants don't have health insurance to protect them if they become sick as a result of the trial or are otherwise harmed by it. Sponsors of clinical trials aren't required to compensate them for any illness or harm that results from the study. The subjects' only recourse in these situations is to hire lawyers and sue in court, a remedy most can't afford.

Yet, those in favor of restricting payments to subjects don't seem to object to another practice: free health care during the trial. Medical help is expensive, and many people enroll in a study just to receive a doctor's care.

Guinea-Pigging

Some healthy people in Phase I trials are professional, paid trial participants who call themselves guinea pigs. They travel from study to study, particularly in cities such as Austin, Texas, and Philadelphia, where many drug companies are located. Guinea-pigging becomes their main job. No data are kept on the numbers of participants who are paid, so no one really knows what percentage of trial subjects are professional guinea pigs.

Professional guinea-pigging raises ethical concerns, particularly in how trials are designed and administered. Most clinical studies for drug tests require that subjects wait a month or more before participating in the next trial. This ensures that drugs offered to the subject in an earlier trial do not affect the current research.

> **NO ONE REALLY KNOWS WHAT PERCENTAGE OF TRIAL SUBJECTS ARE PROFESSIONAL GUINEA PIGS.**

Yet if a guinea pig's incentive is money, that person has every reason to lie about participation in previous or concurrent studies. The subject may have just concluded a study somewhere else or may even be engaged in two trials simultaneously. Sometimes the trial site administrators may bend the rules and allow a particularly likable person to enroll in a second trial. These practices risk contaminating the trial results. They also may harm the health of the guinea pig both in the short and long term.

Workers' Rights

Many critics of medical trials ask why the process of developing new drugs and treatments is considered a moneymaking business for the drug companies, IRBs, CROs, and researchers but not for the participants, who risk the most. Unlike a worker at a fast-food restaurant, guinea-pig participants are not just providing a service in exchange for money. They also are assuming a risk of personal harm on behalf of society.

In most risky jobs, wages frequently are higher than for other jobs, in recognition of more dangerous work. And job benefits, such as workers' compensation for injuries on the job, plus overtime pay, are generally offered as well. Many people feel that clinical trial participants are no different from firefighters or police officers, for whom society does not worry about high pay as a form of coercion.

As some ethicists have noted, perhaps we are simply uncomfortable with the idea of treating experimentation with our bodies as a job.

ANTHRAX SOLDIERS

What rights do U.S. troops in the twenty-first century have to protect themselves against forced medical experimentation? The Pentagon brought this issue to the forefront in a decision in 1997 that mandated anthrax vaccinations for all active and reserve troops.

Anthrax is a deadly bacterial infection. If the bacteria spreads through the skin, the disease often can be treated. But if the spores are released into the air and ingested—as in the case of a biological weapon—the disease is usually fatal. In the 1990s, Pentagon officials were concerned that anthrax could be used for biological warfare in countries such as Iraq and North Korea.

Although the FDA had approved the anthrax vaccination for those at risk, service men and women claimed that it had not been properly tested in battle. Many of those vaccinated had adverse reactions. Technical Sergeant Roberta K. Groll, for example, complained of chronic fatigue, shortness of breath, abdominal pain, and mood swings. By 2000 hundreds of service members were refusing to take the vaccination.

The Uniform Code of Military Justice protects servicemen and servicewomen from forced medical experimentation by requiring informed voluntary consent and prohibiting punishment upon refusal to participate. Those who declined the injections argued that the anthrax vaccine was a medical experiment that they could legally refuse. The Pentagon disagreed and claimed the vast number of vaccinations was administered safely. Officials threatened service personnel with court-martials and discharges with loss of benefits.

Six service members brought a lawsuit to challenge the vaccination program. The court ruled in favor of the vaccination program in 2006, claiming that the FDA had approved the vaccine's safety. Vaccinations are now mandatory for troops and emergency and contractor personnel assigned to U.S. bioterrorism protection and for those serving in Iraq, Afghanistan, or South Korea. It is voluntary for other members of the military.

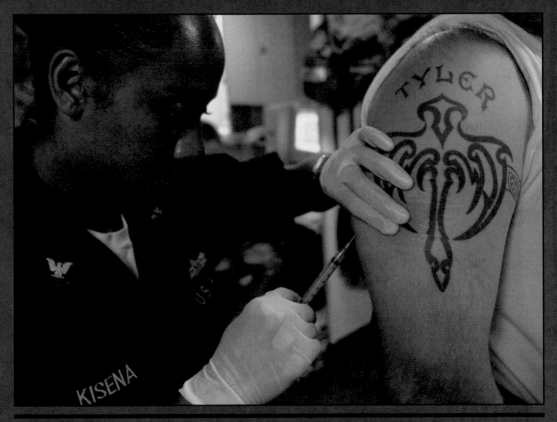

A crew member on board the USS *Mount Whitney* in the Gulf of Aden receives an anthrax vaccine in February 2003. Despite a 2004 lawsuit challenging the vaccination program and lingering doubts about the safety and efficacy of the vaccine, it is currently mandatory for bioterrorism personnel and for members of the military serving in Afghanistan, Iraq, and South Korea.

In most employment, people engage in an active pursuit in exchange for payment. When a person is a research subject, though, actions that can potentially cause harm are being done directly to that person.

Outsourcing Experimentation

Protections for test subjects are no longer just issues for researchers in the United States. The big business of medical research has grown so rapidly that it's almost impossible for clinical trials to find enough American volunteers. For that reason, drug-manufacturing companies are recruiting people from developing countries in Latin America, Asia, and eastern Europe. Financial gain is another factor that drives many drug companies to conduct trials abroad. Citizens in poor nations are more easily recruited and participate for little or no money. The costs of administering studies are less expensive in these nations as well.

In addition, governments of many countries have fewer regulations, so drugs can be brought to market more quickly overseas, earning profits sooner than would be possible if trials were done in the United States. By the early twenty-first century, approximately 40 percent of clinical trials conducted by U.S. companies were administered in developing countries, and the numbers continue to grow.

Oversight in foreign countries is often minimal or nonexistent. IRBs in the United States may approve a trial abroad but may not have supervising staff in the sponsoring foreign country. Companies that conduct research abroad are supposed to follow the Common Rule and FDA regulations.

The All India Institute of Medical Sciences in New Delhi, India, is one of an increasing number of public hospitals in India that gain profits from using their patients to test experimental drugs for markets in the United States and other parts of the Western world. U.S. drug companies outsource medical experimentation to countries where regulations are less rigorous and where it is less costly to conduct testing.

However, monitoring and ensuring compliance at such distances is difficult.

The shift to holding more trials abroad has raised serious ethical concerns. In many countries, health care is poor or nonexistent. People may not have access to clean water or to enough food for their families. In these situations, the lure of free medical treatment and food offered to subjects by the clinical studies outweighs fear of medical risks. Subjects may not even be aware of or understand the potential for financial conflicts among researchers. They may not understand the very nature of research in general. Informed consent is also difficult to ensure abroad. In many developing countries, the head of the community or a religious leader may provide consent for the villagers. Sometimes a husband may give consent for a wife and his daughter. In these cases, individual participants often don't sign consent forms, so it's unclear whether they understand the risks.

Standard of Care

Another ethical question concerns the standard of care for test subjects. Should researchers in international studies provide the standard of treatment that is used in the United States? Or should they use the standard applied in the community where the trial is conducted? The standards are often very different, and a clinical trial for azidothymidine (AZT), a drug for treating HIV/AIDS, brought this issue to the forefront in the 1990s.

At that time, researchers were administering AZT to pregnant women infected with HIV in areas of Africa and Southeast Asia. Researchers knew from experience in the United States that a specific dose of AZT stopped transmission of the virus to newborn babies. But developing countries couldn't afford large quantities of the drug. The trial was conducted to see if a lower dose of AZT would have the same effect.

One group of women received the lower dose of AZT, and a second group received an ineffective pill known as a placebo. Instead of a trial comparing the lower dose of AZT with the standard of care in the United States (the higher dose of AZT), researchers administered the placebo because it was the standard of care in the country sponsoring the trial—that is, no care at all.

Critics were outraged. Since AZT was a known, effective treatment, they thought withholding the drug from women infected with HIV was unethical. Some critics likened the AZT studies to the earlier Tuskegee syphilis trials in the United States, in which black farmers were denied penicillin, the standard of care that would have cured the infected men.

At the time, the AZT trials violated the 1996 version of the Declaration of Helsinki, a set of international guidelines first established in 1964 for conducting medical research abroad. The 1996 version said that researchers could not use placebos when an international standard of treatment—the best-known care worldwide—was known. This held true even when the standard treatment was not used in the country sponsoring the trial. By 2002, however, the declaration had been modified to allow placebos where there is a scientifically compelling reason or where the medical condition is minor and the subject is not at serious risk.

The FDA, however, thought that trials using placebos often produced more reliable evidence. For that reason, the FDA was against international restrictions on placebos. In 2008 the FDA therefore decided that U.S. trials overseas would not follow the Declaration of Helsinki. Instead, the FDA follows practices already adopted in the United States that avoid placebo use when they could cause serious injury. For example, in a study involving a minor condition such as headaches, U.S. researchers might use a placebo because it will not cause serious harm to the subject. On the other hand, researchers would not prescribe a placebo to recent heart attack victims. Yet the FDA's withdrawal has sparked controversy, particularly from supporters of the declaration who had hoped for a global consensus for standard-of-care concerns.

The Nigerian Trovan Experiment

Medical humanitarian crises can lead to exploitation of people in poor countries. For example, a severe, deadly meningitis outbreak in Kano, Nigeria, in 1996 prompted the Pfizer drug company to test a new medication called Trovan (trovafloxacin). One hundred Nigerian children received Trovan while another one hundred children received the standard treatment of ceftriaxone, an antibiotic known to cure meningitis.

Pfizer did not tell the parents or the children that they were part of a research study. The parents thought their children were receiving the standard antibiotic. Five of the children taking Trovan died as did six who took ceftriaxone. Many others in both groups of the study suffered disabling side effects, such as blindness, paralysis, and brain damage.

The parents of the affected children sued Pfizer in the United States. The Nigerian government also brought a legal action against Pfizer in Nigeria. The cases were hard to prove, as the children's hospital records were missing. A written report of an investigation by the Nigerian government had also disappeared.

In 2006 the press uncovered the report, which detailed horrifying ethical violations. Parents of the children who received the standard

Eleven-year-old Firdausi Madaki *(seated on the mat, with her mother)* was one of many children in Kano, Nigeria, to unknowingly receive Trovan as part of a 1996 Pfizer study of the effectiveness of the antibiotic in treating meningitis. Firdausi suffered brain damage and physical disability as a result of the drug. In two separate settlements, Pfizer came to financial agreements to compensate the affected Nigerian families, but it never admitted that the drug was the cause of physical harm and death among the drug-trial patients.

treatment alleged that Pfizer had administered a lower dose of the antibiotic so that Trovan would appear to be the better drug. Pfizer also did not try to save the children who became dangerously ill, either by increasing the dose of ceftriaxone or by switching the treatment from Trovan to ceftriaxone. In addition, a Pfizer researcher had used a fake letter of authorization from a Nigerian ethics committee in support of the study.

Finally, thirteen years after the study was conducted, the victims received justice. Pfizer agreed to pay $75 million to the Healthcare/Meningitis Trust Fund, a board of trustees in Kano charged with administering payment to the victims. Pfizer settled the remaining lawsuit with Nigeria in 2011.

Guatemalan Tragedy

In October 2010, a study in Guatemala came to light through the research of history professor Susan M. Reverby at Wellesley College in Massachusetts. U.S. health officials investigated and discovered that from 1946 to 1948, U.S. public health doctors in an NIH-funded study infected about thirteen hundred Guatemalan soldiers, prisoners, prostitutes, and mental patients with the sexually transmitted diseases syphilis, gonorrhea, and chancroid. In addition, researchers subjected about five thousand of these vulnerable people, as well as orphans, to diagnostic tests for the diseases. The main purpose of the Guatamalan study was to see if penicillin could be administered directly after sex to prevent the development of the diseases. Guatemalan health officials agreed to the study even though it was illegal under Guatemalan law. They viewed the study as a way to improve Guatemalan health care and to learn from U.S. scientists.

Initially, prostitutes already infected with syphilis and gonorrhea were encouraged to have unprotected sex with prisoners and soldiers. When not enough of the men were infected, researchers tried other means. These included inoculations of the bacteria into the spine and swabbing infected solution into the penis and urethra. Mentally ill patients were also subjected to the experiments. Although researchers claimed to have treated most of the subjects, the records suggest that some were only partially treated and others weren't helped at all.

The researchers did not inform the subjects of the testing nor obtain consent from them. One of the public health doctors who led the experiment, John C. Cutler, would later have a lead role in the Tuskegee Syphilis Study. Juan Funes, a public health official in Guatemala, worked with Cutler and supplied the prostitutes.

In response to the public uproar, President Barack Obama telephoned the president of Guatemala to apologize. Secretary of State Hillary Clinton and HHS secretary Kathleen Sebelius issued a joint apology as well.

President Obama asked the Presidential Commission for the Study of Bioethical Issues to investigate the Guatemala case. The commission's final report stated that "the Guatemala experiments involved gross violations of ethics not only in light of modern human research ethics, but also against the researchers' own understanding of medical ethics practices and requirements of the day." The commission also reviewed federal laws protecting human subjects both in the United States and abroad. Among the recommendations for international research, the commission urged further study of the standard of care in foreign studies.

The commission endorsed fourteen changes for stronger protections of human subjects in federally funded studies. One recommendation called for a system to pay those who are harmed. Other important suggestions stressed the need for more oversight, including collecting data on injuries to participants in federally funded studies. The commission also promoted efforts currently under way to amend the Common Rule so that many of the problems affecting the safety of human subjects in the United States and abroad can be solved.

Biospecimens: Yours or Mine?

Human subjects are facing competition as a result of cutting-edge medical and scientific advances. In the twenty-first century, researchers are able to conduct experiments not on live humans but on biospecimens such as human tissue, blood, DNA, and stem cells. Biospecimens contain genes that are passed on from parent to child.

By studying biospecimens, researchers are learning how certain genes are linked to specific medical conditions. Researchers hope to find new ways to diagnose and prevent diseases, discover new gene therapies, and tailor medical care to fit an individual's personal genetic makeup. Researchers refer to these new sciences as regenerative medicine.

Every day, hospitals and clinics across the country collect thousands of tissue and blood samples during surgical procedures and routine doctor visits. Contrary to what many people think, most of these samples are not destroyed. They are housed in laboratories; hospitals; and in research facilities, called biobanks. The U.S. military also stores samples, as do the NIH and the FBI.

For some companies, selling samples for research is a big business. One published report in 1999 stated that biobanks in the United States contained more than 307 million tissue samples collected from more than 178 million people. Use of these samples for medical research raises a host of ethical questions involving privacy, informed consent, and financial gain. Cutting-edge research and new technologies drive novel human experimentation, but the laws and ethical guidelines can barely keep up with them.

Who owns your DNA and blood samples? Do researchers

> IN 1999 BIOBANKS IN THE UNITED STATES CONTAINED MORE THAN 307 MILLION TISSUE SAMPLES COLLECTED FROM MORE THAN 178 MILLION PEOPLE.

need consent to use them? Should businesses be able to reap profits from medical discoveries made with your samples? How can a person's privacy be protected?

Unlike participants in clinical trials, owners of biospecimens do not risk causing physical harm. In this area, the risk is that researchers might hold on to information about an individual without that person's consent or use it for research that the person might find unacceptable.

Cells taken in 1951 from the cervix of Henrietta Lacks while she was being treated for cervical cancer at Johns Hopkins Medical Center became the first human cell line. Known as HeLa, the cells are hardy and replicate quickly and in great numbers. As a result, they are still used in modern medical research around the world. Lacks never gave informed, written consent for the cell harvest, and her family never received financial compensation of any kind.

Henrietta Lacks

In a classic example of biospecimen abuse, doctors at Johns Hopkins Medical Center in Baltimore, Maryland, extracted tissue samples from the cervix of Henrietta Lacks in the 1950s. Lacks was a poor black woman with an extremely aggressive case of cervical cancer. Doctors wanted to study her cancer cells, but they did not seek her consent. Lacks's cells grew and continued to multiply rapidly. Researchers sent the cells to other scientists around the world who were also conducting cancer research. Soon a company called Microbiological Associates began selling the cells to scientists for huge profits.

Lacks's cells, known as HeLa, were used not only for cancer research but also in the development of Dr. Jonas Salk's polio vaccine and in radiation experiments. The cells were even shot into outer space to observe the effects of space travel on cell development. But neither Lacks nor her family ever received a share of the profits.

Duping the Havasupai

Would these events happen in the twenty-first century? Federal laws clearly prohibit extracting samples from a person's body without consent.

But the more difficult issues center on whether people own and control the use of their biospecimens. Courts in the United States say no. For example, once you have consented to a blood test, a biobank owns your collected specimen and can legally sell it.

What about researchers? Does this mean they can do whatever they want with your genes and DNA? The answer depends on the language of the consent form, a subject that is still in flux.

A study involving a small tribe of Native Americans highlighted these problems. In 1990 researchers from Arizona State University collected blood samples from 180 members of the Havasupai tribe, who live at the bottom of the Grand Canyon. Researchers wondered whether genetics played a role in the tribe's high rate of diabetes. Tribe members, anxious to learn why the disease was so prevalent, readily consented.

Although researchers did not find a genetic link to diabetes in the tribe, they continued to use the blood samples for other purposes—without informing the tribe or gaining their consent. The researchers studied the genetic history of the tribe, such as where the tribe originated and how they came to settle in the Grand Canyon. They also tried to find genetic connections in the tribe to a mental disorder known as schizophrenia.

When the tribe learned about the additional research, members were insulted and furious. The studies had concluded that the Havasupai originated in Asia. This contradicted long-held religious and tribal beliefs that they had always lived in the Grand Canyon. Members also felt humiliated by research linking the tribe to mental illness. In April 2010, the university agreed to pay forty-one tribe members for the harm, to build a new health clinic, to give scholarships, and to give back the blood specimens.

Biospecimens and Informed Consent

The Common Rule does not yet address the ethics of biospecimen research, although several organizations have issued guidelines. Many people think consent must be given for each and every use. These individuals don't want researchers using their tissues for studies they find personally objectionable. Many people also think biobanks should ensure privacy so that third parties, such as insurance companies, can't access genetic information. Critics express concern that insurance companies might deny health coverage if they learn of genetic links to certain diseases.

Researchers point to the difficulty of acquiring informed consent for each study involving biospecimens. In many cases, the original source of a biospecimen can't be located or has died. Some sources simply ignore requests for additional authorization.

One suggested solution is to use the generalized consent form required for organ donations. In these cases, people who donate organs for transplants give their organs and tissues as gifts. When signing the form, they consent to all research purposes.

Another solution may be a guarantee of anonymity. Many people don't care what their tissues are used for—as long as no one knows from whom the samples came. In proposed amendments to the Common Rule, the Office of Human Rights Protections (OHRP) recommends "written consent for research use of biospecimens, even those that have been stripped of identifiers." But in the age of the Internet, where privacy is frequently breached, anonymity may be a difficult promise to fulfill.

Stem Cell Research

Stem cell research is one of the most controversial areas of human medical experimentation. Stem cell research involves the study of developing human embryos that are only a few days old. Two moral principles are frequently pitted against each other: the promise of curing terrifying diseases and the experimental use of human embryos, which some people view as potential life.

Most cells in the body are specialized. They develop into only one type of cell, such as skin cells or liver cells. But when an egg and a sperm first join together and form an embryo, the cells have not yet had a chance to specialize. At this early stage, the cells have the potential to grow into any organ in the human body.

Scientists are studying how these young undifferentiated cells, called stem cells, develop. If they can figure out how to instruct these cells before they specialize, they may be able to create specific types of cells that can renew and replace damaged cells in the body that cause disease. Adult stem cells—the older cells that are already specialized—are not as versatile. Although they can repair damaged cells, they appear to be limited in function to the organ or tissue from which they come.

Stem cells also offer another benefit. Once scientists grow the stem cells in a laboratory, the cells can continue to grow for months or even years, becoming a line of stem cells available for research.

Growing a line of human embryonic stem cells is controversial because it involves destroying the embryo when it is two to five days old. The embryo is barely the size of the period at the end of this sentence, and it has yet to specialize into brain, skin, or nerve cells. All the same, inside a woman's womb, it can grow into a fetus and then into a human being.

Many people think embryos, as potential life, are persons and should not be destroyed. Others believe that the benefits of research on embryonic

STEM CELLS ON TRIAL

This scanning electron micrograph (SEM) shows clusters of embryonic stem cells. Advanced Cell Technology is currently the only U.S. company conducting clinical trials with human embryonic stem cells. Consent issues relating to this type of trial are complicated and unresolved. In many cases, forms are signed years before a stem cell study actually launches. Forms from international biotechnology companies are written in a foreign language (requiring translation into English). The forms also typically give consent only for general stem cell research rather than for specific types of stem cell experimentation.

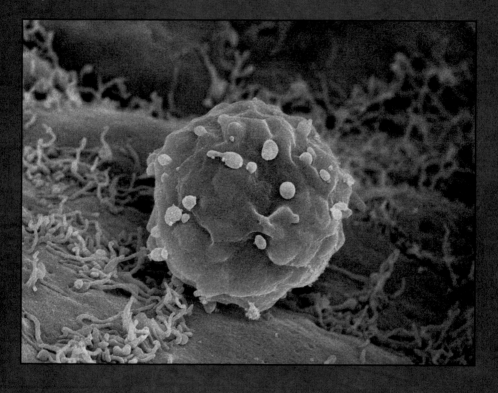

stem cells for future medical treatments far outweigh their destruction.

Another source of embryos already exists in fertility clinics across the United States. Many couples who have trouble conceiving go to fertility clinics. There, doctors can take sperm from a man to fertilize eggs from a woman outside the body. This process is called in vitro fertilization. The fertilized egg is then implanted in a woman's uterus, where it may begin a pregnancy.

Frequently, several eggs are fertilized for the most chances for a pregnancy. The extras are usually frozen. Sometimes they are preserved in case the couple later wants another child. But more often than not, the extras are eventually destroyed. Many couples consent to donate their extra embryos as a source of stem cells for research.

Benefits of Stem Cell Research

Despite the ethical dilemmas posed by experimentation with stem cells, it is a rapidly developing area of research around the world. The Common Rule states that an embryo is not a "human subject" under the law. This means that research may be conducted on stem cells, even if embryos are destroyed. In 2009 U.S. president Barack Obama lifted a prior ban on federal funding for creating new stem cell lines. The embryos must have initially been created in fertility clinics and no longer be needed, and they must have been donated at no charge with the consent of the couple. Researchers of embryonic stem cells predict future benefits from understanding how the human body develops. These benefits might include preventing deformities in fetuses and treating genetic diseases such as juvenile diabetes and Parkinson's disease, a brain disorder.

Someday, stem cell research may also lead to the ability to grow new human organs for safer, more effective transplantations. It may also allow scientists to one day test new drugs on a "disease-in-a-dish" rather than exposing humans to the risks of clinical trials.

Genetic Enhancement

Stem cell research in combination with other technological advances in science may one day enable people to select genetic traits to alter or enhance themselves. Various procedures already exist. For example, athletes take steroids to make themselves stronger and to run faster. People undergo plastic surgery to improve their appearance or to make repairs related to accidents. Others take antidepressants to deal with mood disorders. Are genetic enhancements any different?

When a person opts for self-enhancement, it generally only affects that person. But if parents were able, for example, to change the color of a fetus's eyes or create a more intelligent or artistic child, their decision would also be altering genetic traits for generations to come. For many, this notion of "designer babies" brings back chilling memories of eugenics and the Nazi dream of creating a perfect race. Enhancement may be less objectionable, though, if a fetus were altered to prevent a disabling deformity. Where should society draw the line?

Genetic enhancement must be approached with caution. But the scientific and technological innovations hold promise for improving people's lives. For example, techniques for creating a synthetic eye might help a blind person see. And if stem cells can repair damaged cells, in the future, they might even be able to increase the life span of humans.

Many ethical and legal concerns about human enhancement still need to be addressed. A difficult balance will have to be struck between the rights of individuals to control their bodies and the dangers enhancement might pose to human life as we know it.

Finding a Path to Respect, Beneficence, and Justice

Many of the experiments discussed in this book are not morally justifiable. Individual freedoms we hold dear—such as respect, privacy, and freedom of choice—were violated. Young orphans, without parents to provide care, were exploited for new vaccines. Black slaves were subjected to painful surgeries and displayed in public. Prisoners carried the scars from toxic acids for their entire lives.

During World War II, Nazi doctors committed inhumane experiments on concentration camp inmates with total disregard for the sanctity of human life. American soldiers, who risked their lives for the security of their country, developed cancers from radiation exposure, as

did thousands of innocent people across the United States. Vulnerable people—the elderly, the mentally deficient, the poor, and the uneducated—have all suffered.

These cases serve as lessons. They teach us what happens when the ends—medical advancements—are held up to justify the means. And they set an example for behavior never to be repeated again. People can and do learn from their mistakes.

In the twenty-first century, federal laws are in place to safeguard people enrolled in medical experiments. These laws must be followed strictly and enforced when lapses occur. Studies must be planned so that participants experience the least amount of risk possible. Potential risks must be reasonable when compared to the benefits, and participants must always give informed consent.

But even in our vastly improved research climate, gaps in protection remain. Medical research has become a multibillion-dollar business driven by profit. New medications are often rushed too quickly into clinical trials. IRBs don't exercise enough oversight, and researchers are financially tied to trial sponsors. In practice, informed consent can be an empty promise. Consent forms may be vague, and researchers sometimes hide the truth about the risks and benefits of studies.

What's to be done? The OHRP is studying potential changes to the Common Rule. The new rules, if enacted, will expand coverage to all institutions, such as colleges and universities, that receive any kind of federal funding, even if the specific research is paid for by private sources. This means more people in clinical trials will be protected. The proposed changes will also work to improve IRBs, to create centralized data collection, and to deal more effectively with the explosion of genetic research.

Ultimately, ethical research rests with those conducting the studies. The rules in place are only as effective as those who practice them. Society must decide what standard of care it demands. Will we continue to seek participants among the poor and other vulnerable populations who may be easier to manipulate or deceive? Who should bear the burden of risk for the rest of us?

Medical research ethics test what we think it means to be a moral society. How we treat those who are weakest reflects on who we truly are. Scientific advancement is critical. Without question, society has reaped the benefits from tremendous medical discoveries and treatments. Inevitably, some people will be hurt to save others. In all cases, though, medical research must meet the requirements of respect, beneficence, and justice. How we balance individual rights with the needs of society will demand tough decisions and will define us as people.

This book has described a wide range of unethical and immoral medical behavior on the part of researchers, doctors and other medical staff, and government officials. Many of the people involved in human medical experimentation over time felt they were doing good by advancing the cause of scientific research and medical technology. In some cases, individuals recognized that their decisions and actions were wrong, illegal, or caused immense suffering. However, they felt strongly that other factors were of higher value and worth the risks and the harm inflicted on fellow human beings. Many of the subjects involved in the experiments participated without knowing the full dangers they were facing. In many cases, they were unknowing subjects who never were asked for or gave their consent.

Working with friends or classmates, review the following scenarios and questions. They are all related to the situations you have read about in this book. Discuss the questions together and write down the answers you came up with. Include disagreements. Wrap up the activity by discussing the process. Was it easy or hard to answer the questions? Did your team generally agree or disagree on answers? Why or why not? How might your experience with this activity be similar to what earlier generations faced? How might it be similar to what researchers and subjects are grappling with in the twenty-first century?

Chapter One

Can we judge doctors who practiced medicine in the eighteenth, nineteenth, and early twentieth centuries by today's standards of behavior? Some people say no. They think that we are more enlightened today and have different ideas of what is right and wrong. On the other hand, some argue that despite the lack of formal laws, doctors were obligated to follow ethical standards forbidding abusive experiments. What do you think? Does your answer depend on whether the subjects were slaves or other people who had little control over their lives, such as children or those condemned to death? What about patients for whom there was no cure? Do you think that the lack of understanding of medical science during these years justified relaxed ethical standards in experimentation?

Chapter Two

In reading the Nazi doctors' defenses to abusive medical experimentation, how do their justifications for their actions fall short?

Chapter Three

1. In wartime, many people believe human experiments must be performed. How do you decide which risky experiments are justified for national security purposes? When should wartime experiments be kept secret? Should they be aired in public? How can secrecy in the name of national security affect doctors' judgments?

2. Men and women in the armed forces are asked to sacrifice their lives. Do you think this sacrifice should include exposure to risky human medical experimentation? When do troop exercises, like those at the Nevada Test Site, cross the line?

Chapter Four

Why do you think black doctors did not protest the Tuskegee Syphilis Study? How do you think the history of slavery affected the formation and continuation of the study? Why do you think many African Americans in the twenty-first century do not completely trust medical doctors?

Chapter Five

1. Pharmaceutical companies and academic institutions serve a vital purpose in developing new treatments and medical devices. They also fund important research. Financial gain is involved. How can we balance the responsibilities of researchers to conduct safe and ethical studies with their hope for increased financial support and compensation?

2. The principle of justice in the Common Rule requires that research subjects represent a diverse group of people, by sex, race, and ethnicity, and across all economic and education levels. Do you think payment promotes the idea of justice in human research? Can you think of other ways to promote a diverse group of subjects?

3. If providing benefits to subjects in developing countries can avoid exploiting poor people, what benefits would you provide? Some ethicists think it is sufficient that participants receive free medical care while they participate in the study. Others argue that companies should provide the community with the tested medicines, if they prove successful. Can you think of any other ways that sponsoring companies can give back to a community of volunteers?

4. Scientists are collecting DNA and mapping the human genome

from thousands of people. The results are displayed on websites and accessed by scientists and other people from around the world. Researchers say that more knowledge will promote faster research and cures. One day, having a map of your genome might help treat you and others for a serious disease. How much information would you want others to know about you? Would you want to know that you had a high risk for a disease that currently did not have a cure?

5. Suppose a researcher learned important information affecting your health from studying a tissue sample collected years ago by your doctor. Do you think the researcher should be required to tell you the information? Do you think other family members should be told, as well?

SOURCE NOTES

5 Albert Leffingwell, *An Ethical Problem or Sidelights Upon Scientific Experimentation on Man and Animals*, 2d ed. (New York: C. P. Farrell, 1916), 324.

5 *San Francisco Examiner*, "Mercy Flight Brings Aussie Boy Here: Suffering From Rare Bone Ailment, He Seeks Treatment," April 16, 1946, 1, quoted in Advisory Committee on Human Radiation Experiments, Final Report, Chapter 5, no, 90, n.d., http://www.hss.energy.gov /healthsafety/ohre/roadmap /achre/chap5_2.html (February 13, 2013).

5 Eileen Welsome, *The Plutonium Files: America's Secret Medical Experiments in the Cold War* (New York: Random House, 1999), 152.

5 *New York Times*, "Army and Red Cross Fly an Ill Australian Boy," April 17, 1946.

8 Diana Belais, "Vivisection Animal and Human," *Cosmopolitan*, 1910, 270–71, http://books.google. com/books?id=cJDNAAAAMAAJ &printsec=frontcover#v=onepage &q&f=false (July 31, 2012).

8 Ibid., 271.

9 Jay Katz, "The Consent Principle of the Nuremberg Code: Its Significance Then and Now," quoted in George J. Annas, and Michael A. Grodin, eds., *The Nazi Doctors and the Nuremberg Code: Human Rights in Human Experimentation* (New York: Oxford University Press, 1992), 229.

11 Thomas Percival, *Medical Ethics*, 1846, quoted in Stanley Joel Reiser, "Words as Scalpels: Transmitting Evidence in the Clinical Dialogue," *Annals of Internal Medicine*, 92, no. 6 (June 1980): 837.

11 Sylvio Leblond, "The Life and Times of Alexis St-Martin," *Canadian Medical Association Journal*, 88 (June 15, 1963): 1,206.

13 Harriet A. Washington, *Medical Apartheid: The Dark History of Medical Experimentation on Black Americans from Colonial Times to the Present* (New York: Random House, 2006), 66.

14 Susan E. Lederer, *Subjected to Science; Human Experimentation in America before the Second World War* (Baltimore: Johns Hopkins University Press, 1995), 7.

16 Vivisection Investigation League, *What Vivisection Invariably Leads To*, New York, n.d., quoted in Susan Eyrich Lederer, "Hideyo Noguchi's Luetin Experiment and the Antivivisectionists," *Isis*, 76, no. 1(March 1985): 36, citing .

17 George Bernard Shaw, *The Quintessence of Ibsenism: Now Completed to the Death of Ibsen* (New York: Brentano, 1913), quoted in Jonathan D. Moreno, *The Body Politic: The Battle over Science in America* (New York: Bellevue Literary Press, 2011), 64.

17 *American Medicine*, editorial comment, "Orphans and Dietetics," vol. 27 (August 1921): 396.

18 Diana Belais, quoted in "A Recent Case of Human Experimentation," *Open Door*, November 1915, 4, quoted in Susan Lederer, *Subjected to Science*, 111.

21 Eva Mozes Kor, "The Mengele Twins and Human Experimentation: A Personal Account,"quoted in Annas and Grodin, *The Nazi Doctors*, 58.

21 Ibid., 53.

22 Ibid.

22–23 Ibid., 56.

29 Elie Wiesel, "Foreword," in *The Nazi Doctors and the Nuremberg Code*, ix.

29 Eva Mozes Kor, "The Mengele Twins and Human Experimentation," quoted in Annas and Grodin, *The Nazi Doctors*, 58.

31 Hazel O'Leary, quoted in Welsome, *The Plutonium Files*, 7.

37 Nathan Leopold, *Life Plus 99 Years* (Garden City, NY: Doubleday, 1958), quoted in Allen M. Hornblum, *Acres of Skin: Human Experiments at Holmesburg Prison* (New York: Routledge, 1998), 82.

37–38 Alvin Shuster, *New York Times Magazine*, "Why Human 'Guinea Pigs' Volunteer," April 13, 1958, 62.

40 Clemens Benda to [parent's name deleted], letter, May 28, 1953, in *Task Force, Research That Involved Residents of State-Operated Facilities*, B-23, quoted in Welsome, *The Plutonium Files*, 235.

42 Dennis Domrzalski, "Sailor Spent Two Weeks on Contaminated Ship," *Albuquerque Times*, April 27, 1994, C-1, quoted in Welsome, *The Plutonium Files*, 175.

47 Welsome, *The Plutonium Files*, 424.

47 Ibid., 425.

47 U.S. Department of Energy, Office of Health, Safety, and Security, *DOE Openness: Human Radiation Experiments: Roadmap to the Project, Building Public Trust*, Appendix A, "Remarks By President William J. Clinton in Acceptance of Human Radiation Final Report," 2, 1995, http://www.hss.energy.gov/healthsafety/ohre/roadmap/whitehouse/appa.html (February 14, 2013).

47 Ibid., 3.

47 Corydon Ireland, "U.S. Apology Hits Home," *Rochester Democrat & Chronicle*, December 17, 1996, 1, quoted in Welsome, *The Plutonium Files*, 474.

49 Katz, "The Consent Principle," quoted in Annas and Grodin, *The Nazi Doctors*, 228.

49 Al Zabala, quoted in Hornblum, *Acres of Skin*, 7.

50 Hornblum, *Acres of Skin*, 233.

51 Adolph Katz, "Prisoners Volunteer To Save Lives," *Philadelphia Bulletin*, February 27, 1966, quoted in Hornblum, *Acres of Skin*, 37.

51   Johnnie Williams, quoted in Hornblum, *Acres of Skin*, 120.

51   Ruth R. Faden, Susan E. Lederer, and Jonathan D. Moreno, "U.S. Medical Researchers, the Nuremberg Doctors Trial, and the Nuremberg Code: A Review of Findings of the Advisory Committee on Human Radiation Experiments," quoted in Ezekiel J. Emanuel, Robert A. Crouch, John D. Arras, Jonathan D. Moreno, and Christine Grady, eds., *Readings and Commentary: Ethical And Regulatory Aspects Of Clinical Research* (Baltimore: Johns Hopkins University Press, 2003), 7–8.

53   Rebecca Skloot, *The Immortal Life of Henrietta Lacks* (New York: Random, 2010), 134.

55   Tuskegee Syphilis Study Legacy Committee, quoted in Susan M. Reverby, ed., *Tuskegee's Truths: Rethinking the Tuskegee Syphilis Study* (Chapel Hill: University of North Carolina Press, 2000), 559.

56   National Research Act, Pub. L. No. 93-348, July 12, (1974).

59   Wiesel, "Foreword," ix.

62–63   Jerry Menikoff, *What the Doctor Didn't Say: The Hidden Truth about Medical Research* (New York: Oxford University Press, 2006), 16.

63   Karen J. Maschke, interview, July 25, 2012.

65   Rick Weiss, "Death Points to Risks in Research, One Woman's Experience in Gene Therapy Trial Highlights Weaknesses in the Patient Safety Net," *Washington Post*, August 6, 2007, http://www .washingtonpost.com/wp-dyn /content/article/2007/08/05 /AR2007080501636_pf.html (September 23, 2012).

65   Ibid.

74   Presidential Commission for the Study of Bioethical Issues, *"Ethically Impossible" STD Research in Guatemala from 1946 to 1948*, September 2011, 93, http:// bioethics.gov/cms/sites/default /files/Ethically Impossible (with linked historical documents) 2.7.13.pdf (April 15, 2013).

78   Office for Human Research Protections, "Regulatory Changes in ANPRM: Comparison of Exising Rules with Some of the Changes Being Considered," July 2011, http://www.hhs.gov /ohrp/humansubjects /anprmchangetable.html (June 24, 2012).

80   Insoo Hyun, "Stem Cells," Hastings Center, 2013, http:// www.thehastingscenter.org /Publications/BriefingBook /Detail.aspx?id=2248 (July 25, 2012).

80   Mark S. Frankel and Cristina J. Kapustij, "Enhancing Humans," Hastings Center, 2013, http:// www.thehastingscenter.org /Publications/BriefingBook /Detail.aspx?id=2162 (June 25, 2012).

SELECTED BIBLIOGRAPHY

Annas, George J., and Michael A. Grodin, eds. *The Nazi Doctors and the Nuremberg Code: Human Rights in Human Experimentation*. New York: Oxford University Press, 1992.

Eliott, Carl. *White Coat Black Hat: Adventures on the Dark Side of Medicine*. Boston: Beacon Press, 2010.

Emanuel, Ezekiel J., Robert A. Crouch, John D. Arras, Jonathan D. Moreno, and Christine Grady, eds. *Readings and Commentary: Ethical and Regulatory Aspects of Clinical Research*. Baltimore: Johns Hopkins University Press, 2003.

Hornblum, Allen M. *Acres of Skin: Human Experiments at Holmesburg Prison*. New York: Routledge, 1998.

Jonsen, Albert. R. *The Birth of Bioethics*. New York: Oxford University Press, 1998.

Kaebnick, Gregory E., ed. The Hastings Center Report. Garrison, NY: The Hastings Center 38, 2 (March-April 2008).

Lederer, Susan E. "Children as Guinea Pigs: Historical Perspectives." *Accountability in Research* 10 (2003): 1–16.

———. *Subjected to Science: Human Experimentation in America before the Second World War*. Baltimore: Johns Hopkins University Press, 1995.

Menikoff, Jerry, and Edward P. Richards. *What the Doctor Didn't Say: The Hidden Truth about Medical Research*. New York: Oxford University Press, 2006.

Moreno, Jonathan D. *Undue Risk: Secret State Experiments on Humans*. New York: Routledge, 2001.

Petryna, Adriana. *When Experiments Travel: Clinical Trials and the Global Search for Human Subjects*. Princeton, NJ: Princeton University Press, 2009.

Scott, Christopher Thomas. S*tem Cell Research Now: A Brief Introduction to the Coming Medical Revolution*. New York: Penguin, 2006.

Washington, Harriet A. *Medical Apartheid: The Dark History of Medical Experimentation on Black Americans from Colonial Times to the Present*. New York: Random House, 2006.

Welsome, Eileen. *The Plutonium Files: America's Secret Medical Experiments in the Cold War*. New York: Random House, 1999.

FOR FURTHER INFORMATION

Books

Friedlander, Mark P., Jr. *Outbreak: Disease Detectives at Work*. Minneapolis: Twenty-First Century Books, 2009.

Goldsmith, Connie. *Battling Malaria: On the Front Lines against a Global Killer*. Minneapolis: Twenty-First Century Books, 2011.

Jurmain, Suzanne. *The Secret of the Yellow Death: A True Story of Medical Sleuthing*. Boston: Houghton Mifflin Books for Children, 2009.

Kallen, Stuart A. *The Race to Discover the AIDS Virus: Luc Montagnier vs Robert Gallo*. Minneapolis: Twenty-First Century Books, 2013.

Kor, Eva Mozes, and Lisa Rojany Buccieri. *Surviving the Angel of Death: The True Story of a Mengele Twin in Auschwitz*. Terre Haute, IN: Tanglewood, 2009.

Skloot, Rebecca. *The Immortal Life of Henrietta Lacks*. New York: Random House, 2010.

Uschan, Michael V. *The Tuskegee Experiments: Forty Years of Medical Racism*. Farmington Hills, MI: Lucent Books, 2006.

Websites

Candles Holocaust Museum—Children of Auschwitz Nazi Deadly Lab Experiments Survivors
http://www.candlesholocaustmuseum.org/index.php?sid=26
This museum in Terre Haute, Indiana, was established by Eva Kor and contains educational materials and videos about the Mengele twins and the Holocaust.

Dr. Jenner's House and Museum
http://jennermuseum.com
This website explores the history and science behind Edward Jenner's discovery of the smallpox vaccine.

The United States Holocaust Memorial Museum
http://www.ushmm.org
Extensive information about Nazi medical experimentation is available at this site, including historical footage, information about Josef Mengele

and the twins experiments, testimony from concentration camp survivors, and archival photos.

Films

The Deadly Deception
This documentary, hosted by ABC News medical correspondent George Strait, focuses on the Tuskegee Syphilis Study. It was written, produced, and directed by Denise DiAnni for *Nova* (WGBH Boston) in 1993.

Declassified: Human Experimentation
This 1999 television episode for the History Channel's *History Undercover* series was written and produced by Avner Tavori and Nick Brigden and directed by Avner Tavori. The episode recounts U.S. radiation experiments on soldiers during the Cold War.

Interviews

Allen M. Hornblum (criminologist and author)
http://www.democracynow.org/2000/8/1/holmesburg_prison
Hornblum and Loedus Jones, a victim of experiments at Holmesburg Prison, speak out about inmate experimentation at Holmesburg, with interviewers Amy Goodman and Juan Gonzalez of *Democracy Now!*

Eva Mozes Kor (Mengele twin at Auschwitz)
http://www.youtube.com/watch?v=-gt6UnmjcDo
From Auschwitz to Forgiveness is a thirty-minute interview with Eva Mozes Kor, produced by Dave Taylor (Indiana State University) in 2007. Part of the interview is filmed at Auschwitz.

Susan Reverby (Wellesley College historian and author)
http://www.democracynow.org/2010/10/5/the_dark_history_of
_medical_experimentation
Amy Goodman, interviewer and host of *Democracy Now!*, talks with Reverby about the Tuskegee and Guatemala syphilis studies about which she has written, as well as about other human experimentation.

Harriet Washington (medical ethicist and author)
http://www.democracynow.org/2007/1/19/medical_apartheid_the
_dark_history_of
Amy Goodman and Juan Gonzalez of *Democracy Now!* interview Washington about the history of medical experimentation on African Americans.

Eileen Welsome (Pulitzer Prize-winning journalist)
http://www.democracynow.org/2004/5/5/plutonium_files_how
_the_u_s
With interviewer and host Amy Goodman, Welsome speaks out on
Democracy Now! about radiation experiments in the United States and
the government cover-up.

INDEX

PHOTO ACKNOWLEDGMENTS

The images in this book are used with the permission of: © Joshua Shaw, eldest son to Freda (mother) and brother to Simeon, p. 4; © Hulton Archive/Getty Images, p. 10; © Somers Historical Society, p. 12; Department of Historical Collections and Services/Claude Moore Health Sciences Library/University of Virginia, p. 15; Courtesy Everett Collection, p. 18; AP Photo/CA F pap, p. 20; © United States Holocaust Memorial Museum, pp. 23, 28; © Bettmann/CORBIS, p. 25; American Philosophical Society, p. 27; Ed Westcott/American Museum of Science and Energy/ Wikimedia Commons, p. 30; © Daily Herald Archive/SSPL/Getty Images, p. 34; AP Photo, p. 37; © Stock Montage/Archive Photos/Getty Images, p. 42; © Wally McNamee/Sygma/CORBIS, p. 46; AP Photo/Urban Archives/Temple University, p. 48; © Peter Stacklepole/Time Life Pictures/ Getty Images, p. 53; National Archives/Wikimedia Commons, p. 55; AP Photo/Courtesy Mohr Family, p. 65; © Sean Gallup/Stringer/Getty Images, p. 69; Kathleen Flynn/St. Petersburg Times/Zumapress/Newscom, p. 70; AP Photo/George Osodi, p. 73; © Science Source, p. 76; © Steve Gschmeissner/Science Source, p. 79.

Front cover: © Eric Von Seggern/Shutterstock.com.

Main body text set in Photina MT Std 11/14.
Typeface provided by Monotype Typography.

ABOUT THE AUTHOR

Vicki Oransky Wittenstein has been a prosecutor and an advocate for children and young adults. In 2006 she received her M.F.A. in Writing for Children and Young Adults from Vermont College of Fine Arts. Her first book, *Planet Hunter: Geoff Marcy and the Search for Other Earths*, received the 2011 Science Communication Award from the American Institute of Physics (AIP). She has published many articles in *Highlights for Children*, *Odyssey*, *Faces*, and *The Best of Children's Market*. She and her husband live in Brooklyn, New York, and have two children. You can learn more about her at www.vickiwittenstein.com.